the co-operative movement
in the Netherlands

an analysis

Nationale Coöperatieve Raad

The Hague

1957

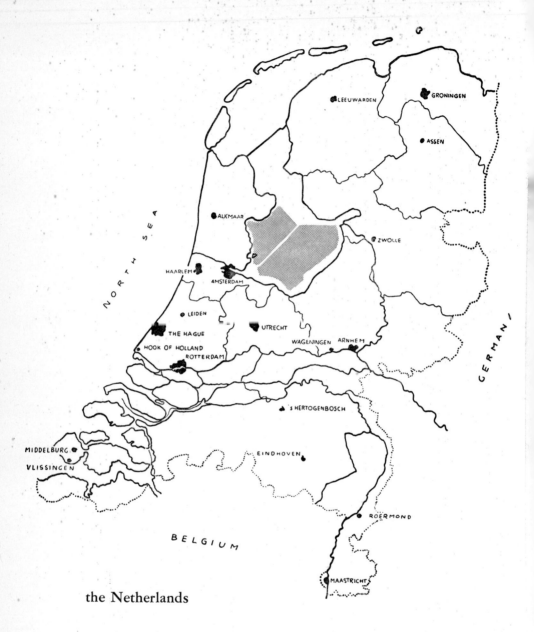

the Netherlands

ultimo 1956:

area 12,529 sq. miles
population 10,957,040
density 874.6 per sq. mile

area under reclamation

0   10   20   30 miles

population active in (1947)

agriculture	19.6 %
industry	36.9 %
trade and communication	23.7 %
other branches and professions	19.8 %

the co-operative movement in the Netherlands

the co-operative movement in the Netherlands

an analysis

Nationale Coöperatieve Raad

The Hague

1957

Foreword to the first edition

The co-operative movement, which sets itself the objective of strengthening the position of economically weaker groups in society, can make a real contribution to the progress of the national community. This has certainly proved true in Western Europe, where the movement has assumed great significance. It applies also to the Netherlands, which, together with a few other western European countries, occupies a place in the front rank as regards progress made in this field. Nowhere is the movement so many-sided as in our small and densely populated country.

Great attention is being paid in the post-war world to ways and means of speeding up economic progress. Since in many countries the idea of co-operation is also looked upon as one of the means that contribute to this end, there is a growing need to get to know what has been achieved elsewhere by adopting this form of collaboration. This need manifests itself not only in a great demand for reading matter on the subject, but also in the ever-increasing number of visitors coming to our part of the world to study the co-operative movement in greater detail.

We were accordingly only too glad to act on a suggestion made by our Ministry of Foreign Affairs that a book be put together that would provide a picture of the co-operative movement as it has developed in the Netherlands. The experience we have gained with visitors from abroad —especially with those coming from countries where co-operation is still in its early stages of development — has taught us that the most important subject for this category of visitors is not a description of the present situation the co-operative movement finds itself in, nor the problems the leaders of the movement are at the moment faced with; they are far more inclined to ask what the circumstances were that led to the founding of co-operative societies in the first place, what difficulties were encountered in the process and how these difficulties were overcome. We have accordingly endeavoured in this publication to provide as good an answer as we can to these questions, allotting generous space to analytical observations and setting the development of the co-operative movement—especially in the agricultural field—against a broader background.

The co-operative movement is an exceedingly complex phenomenon. Not only do its objectives include both economic and social elements, but one does not even always obtain the same answer to the question why co-operative action is regarded as desirable. Moreover, there are several different types of co-operative society, each posing its own problems, and, finally, the development each type has undergone has been determined by the actual circumstances, and these vary considerably as regards time and place.

Notwithstanding this, we are convinced that the experience gained in the field of co-operation in our country can be put at the service of other countries. This in no way implies that we should want to force any particular opinion we may have on the reader, and it is even less our intention to tell others, working under entirely different circumstances from ourselves, what they should do in their

4

own case. This work does not, therefore, claim to provide anything more than an analysis of the development of the co-operative movement in the Netherlands which will make it clearer than do many other publications how greatly the ways of fostering the movement depend on the objective set and the actual circumstances under which one goes to work.

It is hoped that the reader will approach the book in this spirit and that it will contribute towards strengthening his conviction that a co-operative society can only make good progress, if its founders are conscious of the economic and social objectives of the movement, and if they couple faith with a realisation of practical possibilities.

We are most grateful to Miss F. Terlouw, for her part in preparing this book.

Nationale Coöperatieve Raad
H. J. Frietema, *Secretary*

The Hague, December 1956

Foreword to the second edition

We are gratified that this publication should have met with a good reception, from which it is apparent that the analysis provides for an existing need.

In view of the nature of the work, and since only one year has passed since the first impression was issued, we have made no alterations to the text, except for a few changes of minor significance.

Since the chief purpose of the book is to inform those interested concerning the way in which co-operation has developed in the Netherlands, we have no objection to passages being quoted, in order that our experience may be made use of in the work of providing information in other countries regarding the possibilities co-operation has to offer. We shall, however, appreciate it if, when quoting from the work, mention is made of the source from which the quotations have been derived.

Nationale Coöperatieve Raad
H. J. Frietema, *Secretary*

The Hague, December 1957.

Foreword to the second edition

Contents

In this densely populated country intensive use is made of the soil. Horticulture takes place partly under glass

Dairy farming occupies by far the most important place in agricultural production

The reclaimed areas, where crop-farming predominates, are a model of parcelling

chapter I

Introduction

The aim of this publication is to afford the reader an idea of the significance of the co-operative movement in the Netherlands. It does not endeavour to supply full information, supported by a mass of statistics, regarding the size and number of the various forms of co-operative in this country; instead it attempts an analytical approach. In other words, particular attention will be devoted to answering such questions as why it was decided to set up co-operatives, what difficulties were encountered in the process, how far these difficulties have influenced the forms of organisation adopted, why the co-operatives in the Netherlands display such great diversity, etc.

To begin with, in the Netherlands *agricultural co-operatives* have been developed to a far higher degree than have the consumers' co-operatives; moreover, the agricultural co-operatives are divided into various groups, and the problems involved in their establishment and further development vary considerably from group to group. For these reasons, far more space has had to be devoted to the discussion of the co-operative movement in agriculture than to the consumers' co-operatives. The book's composition has also been influenced by a third factor. The origin and development of the *consumers' co-operative* have differed little in the Netherlands from their origin and development elsewhere. For an analysis of the various aspects of the consumers' co-operative the reader can therefore be referred to the general literature on the subject, in particular to the many publications issued in the United Kingdom and Sweden. The development of the agricultural co-operative, on the other hand, has been intimately bound up with the structure of agriculture in the country concerned and consequently presents a different picture in each country, despite the fact that forms of organisation have been based on principles generally accepted in Western Europe, one has only to think, for example, of Raiffeisen's influence. Accordingly, this introduction will begin by presenting an outline of agriculture in the Netherlands and its significance as regards the country's economy.

With regard to the further arrangement of the book, only a few other remarks are necessary in addition to what has already been said. The chapters dealing with the principal forms of agricultural co-operative are followed by a separate chapter on the consumers' co-operatives.

Co-operatives of diverse kinds are dealt with in a chapter entitled "Other forms of co-operative"; these include service co-operatives, i.e. co-operatives providing various services, mutual insurance co-operatives and retailers' co-operatives. Further chapters go into a number of matters of more general nature, which are essential to a proper understanding of the co-operative movement in the Netherlands. Finally, a brief summary is given in the concluding chapter.

The Netherlands is one of the most densely populated countries in the world—it has 11 million inhabitants and the density of population is 875 per square mile—but it is relatively poor in natural resources. Nevertheless, our country is decidedly not an area where the standard of living is low. This is due to the fact that, generally speaking, the available labour force is used to good advantage.

About the middle of the previous century, when our population stood roughly at the three million mark, almost half the population, that is, about 45 %, was employed in agriculture. As the population increased, the relative number of persons employed in agriculture declined—from 30 % in 1900, to 20 % in 1930 and to 19.6 % in 1947, when the last occupational census was held [1]). This means that the greater part of the increase in population was absorbed by other branches of economic activity undergoing expansion, in particular by industry, which provides 36.9 % of the population with employment, and by trade and communications, which employ another 23.7 %. 19.8 % of the population is employed in other occupational categories.

It is true that the proportion of the total working population employed in agriculture has sharply declined, but the actual number of persons earning their livelihood in agriculture has risen by about 40 % since the middle of the previous century.

Although large-scale technical projects have been carried out since then (the bringing under cultivation of peatlands, drainage-works and impoldering), nevertheless, the area under cultivation has increased to a lesser degree than the agricultural population. The increasing density of the agricultural population is the reason why, compared with the situation in most of the other countries of Europe, the average size of farm in the Netherlands is relatively small, being 24.0 acres. Large landownership does not exist in the Netherlands. The number of farms larger than 125 acres is very small, and represents less than 1 % of the total. The total area covered by such farms is only 7 % of the total area under cultivation in our country. On the other hand, 89 % of the

---

[1]) Since that time the percentage of persons employed in agriculture declined further and is now estimated at 12.5.

farms are smaller than 50 acres and 40 % even smaller than 12.5 acres [2]).
The sharp increase in population has given rise to an increasing shortage
of land in our country, which together with the present law of succession
has led to the further splitting up of many farms already small in
acreage.

When land is scarce but labour available in ample quantities, high
labour productivity can only be achieved by the intensive use of what
land there is, which means that a comparatively large amount of labour
must be used per unit of surface. Agriculture in the Netherlands has
accordingly developed strongly in the direction of *labour-intensive
production*.

This is demonstrated in the first place by the high level of Dutch
livestock farming. This sector of agriculture underwent marked development after the notorious agrarian crisis in the 'eighties of the previous
century. At the time, Europe was flooded with cheap grain from
America, which threatened the farmers of our continent with disaster.
Whereas most of the countries in Europe took measures to protect their
farmers against competition from these cheap products from overseas,
the Netherlands and Denmark chose another way. On the basis of this
cheap grain from overseas, both countries proceeded to develop livestock
farming on a considerable scale. This new development was helped
along by the increasing demand for high quality animal produce in the
surrounding countries, where the standard of living was rising sharply
as the result of industrialisation. With the help of raw materials from
abroad, pigbreeding and poultry farming were also considerably
expanded and for these products too a large market was secured abroad.
In short, livestock farming in the widest sense of the word took on the
character of a refining industry in our country. The export of high-
quality, labour-intensive, finished products was built up on the basis of
cheap, labour-extensive fodder crops from abroad.

Dairy-cattle farming, which occupies the most important place in
livestock farming in general, is carried on partly in those areas where
the level of subsoil water provides the natural conditions favourable
to permanent pasture. But about half the total milk supply comes from
the mixed farms in the sandy soil districts. These districts, which constitute
about 2/5 of the land under cultivation in the Netherlands, are barren
by nature but are now important production areas, thanks to the use of

---

[2]) Here it should be remembered that marketgardening, which is pursued on
small undertakings, is of great significance in our country. If we take only
land-users whose main occupation is arable farming or cattle farming, we obtain
the following figures: farms smaller than 50 acres: 86 % of the total; farms
smaller than 12.5 acres: 27 of the total.

artificial fertilizers. In these regions the small farm predominates, and on these farms especially the best possible use of available labour is a condition for the farmers' enjoyment of a reasonable standard of living. Besides cattle farming, pig breeding and poultry keeping in particular make an important contribution to this. The income of many of the small farms in the sandy soil areas is made up of 1/3 from the income from milk, 1/3 from that of pig breeding and 1/3 from that of poultry keeping. Arable farming on these undertakings is devoted almost entirely to the needs of livestock farming, comprising mainly grain and green fodder. It has already been said that a large portion of the fodder used comes from abroad.

In general, labour productivity in the livestock-farming sector is also promoted by very high yields per acre (concentration of a large number of cattle on small areas) and per animal. The average milk yield per cow in the Netherlands is ± 860 gallons a year with a fat-content of about 3.75 %. The average yield per hen has now risen to over 200 eggs per year.

On the undertakings devoted purely to *arable farming* production has also moved in the direction of greater labour intensity. This has resulted primarily in the extension of the acreage producing labour-intensive crops, such as potatoes and sugarbeets. As regards grain crops, apart from having to import large quantities of grain fodder, our country also has to import grain for bread to meet the greater part of the home demand. Although grain is a labour-extensive crop, the acreage devoted to the production of grain has remained fairly stable in the last few decennia. Here we endeavour to achieve the greatest possible yield per man by the systematic increase of production per acre: in the Netherlands yields per acre are among the highest in the world. Moreover, the farmers have devoted their efforts in considerable measure to improving crops, which is also a labour-intensive activity. The export of arable farming crops is also of significance.

Market gardening occupies a place of especial significance in our country. In this sector the average size of undertaking is appreciably below the national average, being only 5.0 acres. By the intensive use of the area available, inter alia by cultivating crops under glass, these small undertakings provide a good living. There is a ready market abroad for high-quality produce in particular, such as early vegetables, tomatoes, grapes and the like.

It is clear from the foregoing that agriculture in the Netherlands is in large measure dependent upon the *world market*. On the one hand for the import of grain fodder, grain for bread and oil-bearing seeds (the last with a view to the home demand for fats), and, on the other hand, for the sale of finished products, which are produced in larger quantities than are required for home consumption. The value of agricultural

12

products exported, however, exceeds that of agricultural imports by a long way. Last year (1956) agriculture provided 35.9 % [1]) of total exports. The livestock-farming sector contributed 48% of these agrarian exports (dairy produce alone accounting for 20%), arable farming 34½ % and marketgardening 17½ %. To illustrate the significance of our country's export of agricultural produce by a few more particulars it may be mentioned that the Netherlands is the world's largest exporter of condensed milk, the second largest exporter of cheese and the third largest exporter of butter. Recently our country has also become the largest exporter of eggs and it is also the largest exporter of seed potatoes.

The pattern of Dutch agriculture has been largely determined by its acceptance of the principle of the *international division of labour*. This process has been helped along to a considerable degree by the country's geographical position, situated as it is amidst other countries where industry is highly developed and which accordingly form a favourable market for Dutch agricultural and market-gardening produce. For our small and densely populated land especially, participation in international trade is a condition of survival, for it is only thereby that its abundant labour supply can be employed so as to ensure a high standard of living.

This development has only been made possible by the high standard of *proficiency and technical knowledge* among Dutch farmers. The fact that in the 'eighties of the previous century the Netherlands government preferred free trade to protection does not mean that attempts have not been made to improve conditions for agriculture in other ways. This the government did, inter alia, by systematically extending general education, by technical training and by providing a great deal of advice and information on agriculture. But it also called on the farmers *to use their own initiative,* and the farmers had begun to realise as a result of the agricultural crisis that farming in the Netherlands could, indeed, be improved in many respects. One of the most important actions taken by the farmers at the time was the establishment of *agricultural co-operatives.* There is no doubt that as far as the Netherlands are concerned the well-known German saying that agricultural co-operatives are "the children of distress" is true. At the end of the previous century there was a great deal of distress among the farmers; thanks partly to the co-operatives, they were not only able to overcome the consequences of this serious agricultural crisis, without any financial aid from the government, but since then they have also succeeded in gradually improving their social and economic position.

---

[1]) This figure relates to agricultural exports both processed and unprocessed and includes the export of products of foreign origin. Agricultural products of Dutch origin account for 29.3 %.

chapter II

Agricultural credit co-operatives

In the 'eighties of the previous century the Netherlands government set up a special commission to inquire into the state of Dutch agriculture, which, due in part to the agrarian crisis, was most unsatisfactory. The commission was of the opinion that one of the main obstacles in the way of better farming was the lack of credit facilities.

With agricultural credit, as with credit used in other branches of economic activity, a distinction needs to be made between long-term, short-term and medium-term credit. The demand for long-term credit, used to finance fixed assets, such as land, farm buildings and permanent equipment, is usually met by money loans on mortgage, if the provider of the money can be offered adequate security. Although the commission mentioned above could not escape the conclusion that the supply of this type of credit was in some respects unsatisfactory, the rate of interest charged often being too high, it was of the opinion that the supply of working credit, i.e. short or medium-term credit to finance the expansion of the cattle herd, as well as requisites, agricultural machinery, the harvest and the like, was a matter of far greater urgency.

In most cases the farmer had to go to the trader for this type of credit. The power the latter so obtained over the farmer enabled him to secure the interest on such loans largely via the prices he charged for the farming requisites the farmer bought or via the prices he paid for produce delivered by the farmer. The way these prices were fixed left much to be desired in other respects too, so that generally speaking the farmers paid too much for the goods they needed and received too little for the products they themselves supplied. This dependence on the trader and the prevalence of exorbitant rates of interest the commission declared to be serious abuses, which naturally had an unfavourable influence on the standard of farming.

To meet the requirements, the commission recommended the establishment of credit co-operatives, and the farmers, though at first with some hesitation, acted upon its suggestion. The first farmers' credit bank in our country was set up in 1896 on the model developed in Germany following the Raiffeisen system. Whereas in parts of the country membership was also open to the village retailers, other banks of this kind restricted membership to farmers and market gardeners. As a result,

14

the latter had less of the character of village banks than had the Raiffeisen banks in Germany. But apart from this they operated according to the same principles. Since membership of this second group of banks has recently been made open to everyone, the difference is becoming of decreasing significance.

In order to form a good understanding of the significance the credit co-operatives have acquired, it is necessary to go rather further into the special demands put on the supply of short and medium-term credit in agriculture.

The demand for this sort of credit in agriculture displays a great deal of variety, in the first place because a large number of small farms are involved, and also because it is often a question of only small amounts per farm, the actual size of each amount fluctuating with the course of the production process. Moreover, the amount of credit the farmer can be allowed will depend above all on his personal qualities as an entrepreneur. If, however, a farmer's inability to repay a loan on time is due to uncertain natural circumstances, it is only reasonable that the conditions on which the credit is granted should be applied with a certain flexibility. In short, the need for this working credit should be supplied according to a system which takes considerable account of the individual circumstances of the borrower.

The commercial banks, which grew rapidly in importance during the second half of the previous century, were not able to meet the highly decentralised and varied credit requirements of agriculture. It is true that they had a limited number of branches in the provinces, but branch banks, after all, always operate according to set instructions, which leave insufficient latitude for taking the individual circumstances of the borrower into account, when considering applications for a loan. What is more, these banks were far more interested in other branches of economic activity, such as industry and trade, which have expanded increasingly since the end of the previous century.

Short-term loans from private lenders have played a role in agriculture from of old. In these cases it was easy to meet the special demands of this type of credit and the lenders were also able to take sufficient account of the borrower's individual circumstances. But this form of credit, too, could only be on a limited scale, since it was usually of local character only. Then again, private lenders were more interested in loans on mortgage, while they were being increasingly attracted by more profitable investment opportunities outside the agrarian sector.

It can indeed be said that in our country the farmers' credit banks have succeeded in meeting the demand for working credit in agriculture, and this form of co-operation can rightly be termed co-operation based on mutual aid. For the farmers' credit banks can only perform their function insofar as they have the necessary money at their disposal, and this money is supplied in the form of savings and deposits made by country people, who have generally accepted the farmers' credit bank as their savings bank. They appreciate having a savings bank in the village, where they can always deposit their surplus money and withdraw it, when required; for otherwise it would mean waiting until they could make the journey to some regional centre. It is a condition for the functioning of the bank as a savings bank, however, that the saver should have great trust in it. Confidence in the farmers' credit banks rests on the fact that membership involves *unlimited liability* for all the bank's financial commitments, which means that by joining, one becomes, with all one possesses, a guarantor for the good functioning of the bank. In other words, the soundness of these banks is equal to the total financial capacity of its members. In most villages the farmers and market gardeners are practically all members, while other villagers have also joined. This provides savers with sufficient security. For in our country membership of these farmers' credit banks has not remained limited to those who have little or nothing to lose and whose chief reason for joining was to obtain loans on advantageous terms; the more well-to-do have also accepted membership and their liability has greatly strengthened the banks' financial soundness.

Co-operation of this kind, within the framework of the village community, is an essential condition for the functioning of these banks. In our country such co-operation has been aided by various circumstances. In the first place, class differences are not very pronounced in rural areas in the Netherlands. The greater these are, the less willing the "haves" usually are to join credit co-operatives to help the "have-nots". In the second place, there is no doubt that leading personalities in the villages had a great sense of responsibility, and this feeling of solidarity with the farming class or even with the villagers as a whole caused the more well-to-do to become members of the farmers' credit banks and to accept unlimited liability. The church also contributed its share by persuading its disciples that is was their moral duty to help the less well-off as far as they could. In the third place, a very human emotion, love of social distinction, has also lain behind willingness to support the work of the banks by becoming members. In the early stages, in fact, it was leading farmers or leading personalities in the village who became the members of the board and they were proud to do so.

But the success of the farmers' credit banks does not depend only on the amount of savings deposited with them, but also, and particularly, on the sound administration of the funds entrusted to their care. The farmers' credit banks have also been able to meet this demand, due primarily to the principle of *decentralisation*.

16

In most cases the area over which a farmers' credit bank operates is confined to the village; sometimes there are even two such banks in one village. There are more banks than municipalities in our country. Accordingly the average number of members per bank is also small, being about 265. This decentralisation is a condition for the good functioning of a farmers' credit bank. For it is only within the framework of the village community, where everyone knows everyone else, that it is possible to judge whether, on the basis of his personal capacities, a man deserves to be granted credit, and to what extent special circumstances justify its being granted on lenient terms.

A farmers' credit bank will not, however, grant credit without security. This security may take the form of collateral (a mortgage, stocks and shares or other securities, transfer of dead or live inventories), or be personal in nature, whereby two persons, accepted as guarantors by the bank, agree to stand surety for the repayment of the loan on the conditions stipulated. Surety has played a great part in the development of the farmers' credit banks. In the early stages in particular, great use was made of this form of security, and naturally all the more recourse was had to it, where the farmer had already taken out a mortgage on his fixed property. Moreover, the surety system makes it possible for tenant farmers, who can offer no collateral in the form of a mortgage, to receive credit from the farmers' credit banks. The surety system has, indeed, retained its significance to the present day, especially for short-term loans involving only small amounts. For surety too, knowledge of the personal circumstances of the guarantors is also necessary, and it is easier to form a correct opinion on this matter, if one is acquainted with local conditions.

A small operational area is, moreover, a condition for effective control on the use to which credit is put. Farmers' credit banks, as a matter of fact, limit themselves to the granting of *credit for productive purposes*. In order to receive credit the farmer must accordingly be able to show that the amount asked for can be put to use for the running of his farm. It is perfectly easy to exercise control over the manner in which the loan is used: farming is like a house of glass and it is a simple matter to ascertain whether the credit granted is actually being used in accordance with the conditions laid down.

The granting of credit is a task for the members of the board of the farmers' credit bank, which board is composed of members of the co-operative, that is to say, of farmers. Although the circumstances mentioned above facilitate the consideration of requests for credit, it is, of course, essential that in granting it the necessary objectivity should be observed. This demands on the one hand an ability to refuse applications, and only those who have attained a certain independence of judgement can be expected to do this. Another factor making for caution in management, however, is that, as members of the bank, the board members themselves bear unlimited liability for the co-operative's commitments. This withholds them from making free with the funds entrusted to their administration.

Savings can be deposited with the bank by members and non-members alike. The banks pay an attractive rate of interest on deposits. Credit, however, is granted to members only, and the rate of interest charged on such credit is as a rule low. This is possible because the farmers' credit banks operate at low cost. They have no need of attractive and expensive premises. In fact even today some of the banks have no special building of their own, the work being done in the private house of one of the members of the board or of the cashier, in which case the bank is often open a few hours a day only. Generally speaking, board members receive no remuneration at all; the person performing the duties of cashier—often a board member in former times but now usually a special official—receives an allowance. The cashier of a fairly large bank, in full-time employment, receives a salary. Other running costs are also small. Moreover, the fact that credit co-operatives do not aim at making a profit makes it possible for them to charge only low rates of interest for the credit they grant. The margin between interest received and interest to be paid usually leaves some surplus, after the necessary costs have been deducted. Any such surplus may not be distributed among the members of the bank but has to go into reserve. This policy considerably strengthens the solidity of the banks, since in the event of failure, this reserve can be called on before resort is had to the members' liability.

But it is not only the principle of decentralisation that has had a favourable bearing on the development of the credit co-operatives. Their success is also the result of the activity of the *central banks* established by the local farmers' credit banks. Only two years after the first of such banks had been established in our country, the need for a central organisation was felt. In the Netherlands there are two of these central banks, one at Utrecht and the other at Eindhoven. The reason for this can be found in chapter IX.

These central banks have assumed a great importance and there are many sides to their work. In the first place, they act as a clearing house for the local banks. The fact that the local banks operate over a restricted area involves the disadvantage that it is sometimes difficult to maintain a proper equilibrium between available savings deposits and loans issued. The whole system of the farmers' credit banks became far more effective by making surpluses held by some of the banks available to others, unable to meet requests for loans out of their own funds. This was done via a central organisation. Moreover, local banks with a permanent surplus had to look for a good means of investing this. The

18

members of the board had little knowledge of the possibilities open to them in this respect, and a central organisation was in a far better position to maintain contact with the money and capital market. The central banks also advise the local banks regarding legal, organisational and administrative matters.

As the system of farmers' credit banks developed, the influence exerted by the central banks on the management of the local banks increased, and the independence of the latter has been curtailed in some fields. Thus the local banks cannot bring about alterations in the statutes without the approval of the central banks; they cannot grant credit above a certain amount to a borrower without the central bank's permission; the appointment of cashiers has to be approved by the central banks. In addition, the central banks exercise close control over the administration of the local banks. Their inspectors visit them regularly and carry out a thorough inspection of the management. The system of bookkeeping employed by the local banks is uniform, being laid down by the central banks.

With a few exceptions, the local banks are all members of one of the central banks. Unlike the local banks, the central banks work with share capital, which is apportioned among the local banks, the share of each bank being determined by its size. The liability of the local banks for the transactions of the central banks is limited, though it exceeds the amount of their shares; the extent of this excess is not, however, the same in the case of the two central banks.

The farmers' credit banks have developed to form an important section of Dutch banking, both as savings banks and as loan banks. At the end of 1956, $\pm 40\%$ of the total savings deposited with savings banks in the Netherlands (including the Post Office Savings Bank) had been entrusted to the keeping of farmers' credit banks. It can be taken for granted that the amount of credit issued by the farmers' credit banks as a whole exceeds the total granted by the four largest commercial banks in our country, taken together.

Although savings deposited with the banks can be withdrawn on demand, in practice a portion of them remains deposited with the banks over long periods. And since this has been found to be so, the farmers' credit banks have taken to granting long-term loans on a limited scale. Originally they confined themselves to loans secured by mortgage and granted to individual members. As savings began to exceed the demand for loans to an ever increasing degree, the banks also took to granting credit to local co-operatives. In this way the farmers' savings could be employed to aid their other activities. Since the granting of long-term credit to commercial undertakings demands great prudence, the central banks considered it desirable to make loans to large (principally regional

19

or national) co-operatives mainly their own concern. The central bank at Utrecht has set up a separate bank to handle the granting of long-term credit to co-operatives, which bank works to some extent on the basis of debenture loans. The central bank at Eindhoven has also set up a subsidiary bank, especially for dealing with loans on mortgage to its members. Such loans are also issued, though on a modest scale only, by the local farmers' credit banks. Although the financing of co-operatives by the farmers' credit banks is of great significance quantitatively, the amount of loans on mortgage granted by these banks is only of minor importance, when viewed in relation to the total amount of mortgages outstanding in our country.

Although the amount of credit granted by the farmers' credit banks has undergone a considerable absolute increase, as a result of a relatively greater increase in the volume of savings ever larger surpluses have accumulated at the local and central banks. The local banks and their central organisations rely on the money and capital market for the investment of these surpluses, investment policy being the particular concern of the central banks.

Many local farmers' credit banks of any size now perform all manner of banking services for their members.

There are two important co-operative institutions which cannot be regarded either as local farmers' credit banks or as central banks. These are the dairy-farming banks established at Alkmaar and Leeuwarden, the latter being by far the more important of the two. The members of these co-operative dairy-farming banks are local co-operatives (not farmers' credit banks), the chief among them being the co-operative dairy factories. Large sums are deposited with these banks, enabling them to grant loans, which they do to co-operatives in particular. Moreover, these banks perform all sorts of banking services for their members.

There can be no doubt that the farmers' credit banks have made a considerable contribution towards improving the position of the farmer. They have made the farmers independent of loans from traders and industrialists, thereby freeing them from the onerous conditions previously attached to borrowing.

However, the farmers' credit banks have sometimes come in for criticism in times past. This criticism concerned both their soundness and their liquidity. As regards their soundness, the critics were of the opinion that the members' unlimited liability could not be regarded as as adequate a guarantee for the creditors as the possession of capital. As regards liquidity, they expressed the fear that if the banks had to call in loans to meet demands for withdrawals of deposits, the process of collecting the money required from the borrowers would take too much time.

As a matter of fact, the one-sided character of the farmers' credit banks was, in general, regarded as risky. For the banks attract savings from the rural population on the one hand, and, on the other, use these savings to grant credit mainly to the producers of agricultural goods. If the countryside were to be hit by a depression, this—it was contended— would inevitably lead to the large-scale withdrawal of deposits and to a general collapse of the system of credit. Moreover, it would be all the more difficult for members to meet their obligations to the banks, because borrowers from the farmers' credit banks are often each other's sureties.

There can be no doubt that if the farmers' credit banks had had to make a call on their members' liability shortly after they had been established, they would have landed in difficulty. Their success is therefore partly due to the favourable economic situation that prevailed during the first decades of their existence. When a depression did come in the 'thirties, the banks had acquired so great a stability that they were never really threatened. The amount of savings withdrawn was not excessive, and when the depression continued, the farmers began to farm their land less intensively, with the result that the demand for farming requisites fell off.

Since those days increasing attention has been devoted to stability and liquidity. Much greater reserves have been built up, and as a result of the growth in size of the local banks the central banks' share capital has been extended. The size of the local banks incidentally determines the number of shares they have to take in the capital of the central banks. Moreover, the caution that good banking policy demands with regard to the granting of credit has been well and truly applied. Even without taking unlimited liability directly into account, it can be said without any reservation that the farmers' credit banks represent a solid and an important branch of banking in the Netherlands.

chapter III

Co-operatives for the purchase
of agricultural requisites *(supply co-ops)*

The fact that the greater part of agricultural production takes place on small farms and that most of these are many-sided in character means that the farmers come to the market with only small quantities of products covering a wide range; also that they usually purchase only small quantities of the various farming requisites. As a result of this, the farmer is often in a weak position for bargaining. His partners on the market generally represent larger units and owing to their specialisation know more about the state of the market and are better informed about the nature and composition of certain goods, artificial fertilizers and feed-stuffs in particular.

It is usually a difficult matter for the farmer to begin by making contacts with different dealers in order to form an idea of the market before selling his produce or before purchasing the things he needs for his farm. In practice, he accordingly relies on the local dealer, which means that there is insufficient competition between dealers. This can easily lead to dealers earning their money without really serving the interests of their customers. In other words, the dealer is not obliged by strong competition to give service as regards quality, terms of delivery and so on. The situation is all the more difficult when it concerns products whose quality cannot be judged at a glance, as, for instance, in the case of fertilizers and feedstuffs.

As was already mentioned in the introduction to this book, since the 'eighties of the previous century agriculture in our country has been increasingly intensified, a process which has manifested itself especially in the ever-increasing use of *artificial fertilizers and feedstuffs*. As regards these products the Dutch farmer found himself in the situation sketched above: he found it particularly difficult to judge the quality of fertilizers and feedstuffs. It is true that even in those days he could have a sample of the fertilizer he had purchased examined by a state agricultural experimental station, but little use was made of this opportunity. In the first place the farmer bought small quantities of fertilizer at one time. Moreover, even if it proved that he had been supplied with a quality that dit not come up to the stipulated requirements, the result of the examination was of little assistance to him, should he put in a complaint to the dealer. As regards feedstuffs, similar difficulties were encountered when more of this began to be bought in the form of mixed feed. It is not possible to judge the composition of this at sight, and trade in this product was likewise a matter of good faith. In these circumstances there was a great temptation for the dealers to "fiddle" with the quality of the feed delivered, and accordingly the farmer repeatedly found that he had to pay a high price for inferior goods.

It must also be remembered in this respect that artificial fertilizers were a new product, the use of which depended on the results obtained. Should a farmer be disappointed with the results, he was naturally less inclined to listen to advices to use fertilizer, and his disappointment also had its effect on neighbouring farmers.

It was in 1877 that a group of farmers in the south-west of our country first decided to buy the fertilizer they required on a co-operative basis. By purchasing large quantities at a time they not only aimed at creating greater equilibrium on the market but also hoped to profit by rebates, the benefit of which they would enjoy collectively. Moreover, there would be a considerable saving in the cost of transport, if delivery to their village took place in one large consignment. Joint purchase would also enable them to exercise better control on the quality of the fertilizer delivered.

The way this *first co-operative purchasing society* went to work was exceedingly simple. Periodically orders were taken from the members for the quantities of *artificial fertilizer* they required. Then the wholesale trade was invited to make tenders for the delivery of the total amount, the order usually being given to the lowest tenderer. On the arrival of the consignment in the village, all the members were present to receive their share, payment being made in cash. The secretary of the society settled the account with the supplier, after ascertaining that the quality of the consignment was the same as that of the sample offered with the tender. This arrangement did away with the need for a storehouse and staff, and neither had the co-operative any need for working capital. Since each transaction was settled separately, there was even no objection to the society doing business without being incorporated.

The example set by these farmers was soon followed elsewhere in their province, and these "supply co-ops" also began to develop in other agricultural areas as well. Moreover, they did not confine their activities to the purchase of fertilizers; in fact, in some areas the purchase of *feedstuffs* was their main concern.

With the intensification of agriculture, mentioned earlier on in this chapter, the trade in fertilizers and feedstuffs took on ever larger proportions. The supply co-ops succeeded in securing a large share of this trade for themselves, especially because their members could be certain that products obtained via the co-operative were up to standard as regards quality.

As the supply co-ops expanded, an increasing need was felt to *anticipate the members' demand*. This was particularly the case with regard to feedstuffs. The demand for this product is spread far more evenly throughout the year than is the demand for artificial fertilizer. Moreover, the system of purchase, being the same as had originally been followed in buying fertilizers, orders for the total amount required for the whole season being made only once or twice a year, could only be successfully applied in areas where the farmers could pay for large consignments in a lump sum.

In addition, the supply co-ops gradually expanded their activities with regard to *miscellaneous products*. Nowadays, in addition to dealing in fertilizers and feedstuffs — which are still, however, the most important articles they are concerned with — the co-operatives also deal in seeds and seed potatoes, insecticides, fuels, oil and agricultural tools, implements and machines.

The purchase of *seeds and seed potatoes* is just as much a matter of good faith as is the purchase of artificial fertilizers and cattle-feed. In our country a bona fide trade in seed and seed potatoes is furthered by the existence of a national inspection service, whose seal is a guarantee of good quality. But this does not mean that the co-operative has no task to fulfil in this respect, for it can do a great deal to promote the use of good seeds and seed potatoes by providing its members with advice and information. In our country the supply co-ops do not limit their activities to the purchase of seeds and seed potatoes on behalf of their members; they are themselves active in the field of seed improvement on their own nursery farms, set up specially for the purpose.

The co-operatives have also successfully undertaken the purchase of *agricultural tools and implements*. The co-operative purchase of *farming machinery,* on the other hand, is only on a limited scale in our country, in contrast, for instance, to Germany. There are several reasons for this. In the first place, the average size of farm is small in Holland. Besides this, up to the last war agricultural wages were comparatively low, a factor which naturally impeded mechanisation. Since the war, however, mechanisation has made rapid progress, due especially to an increasing shortage of labour in certain regions of the country. For the rest, the purchase of agricultural machinery for individual use remains limited for the most part to the larger farms, while the small farmers attempt to take advantage of mechanisation with the aid of the agricultural machinery co-operatives (see chapter VII). Another obstacle to the development of co-operative purchase in this field is the

24

The Netherlands are covered
by a network of credit co-operatives

One of the local co-operative banks, of which there are about 1300 in the Netherlands

A regional supply co-operative

fact that agriculture in the Netherlands is highly varied in nature. It is not only the large variety of products, which differ from district to district, but also the great diversity in types of soil, which makes it necessary for the purchasing co-operatives to be able to supply many different sorts of farming machinery and accessories, if they are to meet their members' needs. This means that the co-operative purchase of agricultural machinery enjoys the advantage of large-scale transactions to a limited degree only. Moreover, the co-operative's activity in this field is hampered by the fact that the manufacturers of certain makes of machine have entrusted their sale to established private dealers and importers. The latter often raise objections to the manufacturers maintaining relations with the co-operatives, thus permitting the co-operatives to deal in the same make of machine. And as long as the turnover of agricultural co-operatives dealing in farming machinery remains small, the manufacturers are not usually inclined to jeopardise their established relations with private traders.

Over and above this, the development of co-operative dealing in farm machinery in our country strikes up against yet another special difficulty. Here, in the Netherlands, the village smiths often act as the agents for private dealers and importers of farm machinery. As a consequence, they not only have an interest in the sale of the makes put on the market by these private dealers and importers, but, in dealing with repairs, they give priority to machines they have helped to sell. This means that farmers who have bought machinery from a co-operative are more or less dependent, when it comes to repairs, on the village smith's willingness to assist them. A satisfactory solution to this difficulty could be found either in whole-hearted co-operation on the part of the smiths, which at the moment they are not ready to give (they are well-organised), or by establishing a decentralised network of repair stations, which, of course, would also involve difficulties. Despite the difficulties the co-operative purchase of farm machinery has come up against, it has nevertheless shown favourable development in recent years.

The purchase of *fuels* covers fuel for members' domestic use as well as fuel for farming purposes.

In recent times the supply co-ops have also successfully undertaken the purchase of *oil*, the demand for which from members is continually increasing, parallel with the progress of mechanisation in farming. A portion of these oil products are obtained, via an international co-operative sales organisation, the International Co-operative Petroleum Association, from the Co-operative Consumers Association in Kansas (U.S.A.), wich operates large oil-wells and refineries of its own.

Although as the activity of the local supply co-ops grew, an increasing need was felt to set up a *central body* for the joint purchase of farming requisites, the first attempts in this field were hesitant in character. Strong encouragement was given, however, when, at the end of the previous century, Dutch importers of fertilizers formed themselves into a cartel, thus cutting out competition altogether, the prices of fertilizer being dictated by the cartel. To break this monopoly, a central purchasing organisation was set up, which successfully took over the buying of fertilizers. The purchase of cattle-feed soon became part of its business, and its range of products gradually widened, as the demand of the local supply co-ops increased.

This central organisation has developed vigorously. Originally it was the only central organisation in existence and its work covered the entire country. Later, about the year 1920, a group of local co-ops affiliated to the central organisation via regional organisations, seceded from the central organisation, owing to differences in outlook on life. In this way, the principle of organisation on the basis of belief and philosophy, a principle which finds its expression in many fields in our country (see chapter IX), was applied in more consistent fashion. These regional organisations in their turn work together in a central organisation. The large majority of supply co-ops are affiliated to one of both central organisations.

The supply co-ops have gradually come to occupy a position of considerable importance. At the moment more than half of the fertilizers and feedstuffs for cattle and poultry used by the farmers are obtained via the co-operatives. Many local and regional co-operatives have their own silos, and several of them run their own factories for milling and mixing fodder. Both central organisations have large feedstuff factories, which are used chiefly by local co-operatives having no milling and mixing installations of their own.

Originally the supply co-ops restricted their activities to purchase on behalf of their members. Gradually, however, various supply co-ops have also concerned themselves with the *marketing* of their members' produce, so that many of these co-operatives are dualistic in character. The central organisations also lend their services in this field. This section of the supply co-ops' activities is becoming of increasing importance. The goods marketed are chiefly grain crops, agricultural seeds and seed potatoes. For the marketing of other agricultural produce the farmers join specialised marketing co-operatives (see chapter IV).

It has already been mentioned in the foregoing pages that the first supply co-ops were organised on simple lines and that many of them did not have any business organisation to speak of, or any permanent staff. With the passing of the years great changes have come about in this respect. Nowadays practically every supply co-op in our country can boast a well-regulated organisation. As a result, the unincorporated co-operative society is now a rare exception.

This process of development has not been without its consequences.

In the first place, the question arose as to *what price* the members ought to pay for the farming requisites obtained from the supply co-op. The early co-operatives were run on such simple lines that this difficulty did not arise. Immediately the dealer had delivered his consignment, each member paid his share of the sum due, plus his share of the administrative costs, which, however, were always small. When the co-operative proceeded to anticipate its members' demand, this meant that it had to maintain stocks, out of which small consignments were made available to the members at intervals. If the co-operative were always to charge the members the price it had itself paid, this would mean that it transferred the risk involved in its purchasing policy to its members. It would be difficult to persuade members to pay the co-operative the price it had paid, if the market price on the day they made their orders stood considerably below this price. For this reason the co-operatives soon adopted the policy of always charging their members the market price reigning on the day of delivery, as a result of which the co-operative and not the individual member bears the price risk. It is obvious that such a policy is only possible, if the co-operative's financial position permits. In other words, there must be sufficient reserves to meet such risks.

In the second place, a co-operative run as a regular business involves *a greater need for capital*, since the maintenance of stocks requires investment, this partly in connection with the necessary storage space. In addition to this, the increasing demand for mixed feedstuffs gave rise to a need for milling and mixing installations. The increasing use of cattle-feed cakes of diverse composition, according to the type of cattle, saw the establishment of feedstuff factories. As a result of this many supply co-ops expanded to become large undertakings, employing large permanent staffs. Naturally, it was necessary to appoint a manager to be responsible for the day-to-day administration. The increasing need for capital was met in part by building up the co-operative's own capital. This capital was obtained by taking writeoffs and reserve funds into account, when determining the prices members had to pay. Insofar as this was insufficient, the necessary working capital was obtained via loans made to the co-operative on the basis of its members' liability, which was usually unlimited. It cannot be denied that in the case of some local supply co-ops the building up of their own fund of capital leaves something to be desired. The central organisations have been at pains to build up their own capital from the very beginning and have grown to become undertakings with great financial resources. Local co-operative societies have a limited liability towards the central organisations.

The supply co-ops have greatly strengthened the Dutch farmer's position on the market. Their activities have had a favourable effect on the price of the various farming requisites. An especially important factor is the *propaganda* for the greater and more rational use of artificial fertilizer and cattle-feed which the co-operatives have carried on among their members. The effect of this propaganda has been considerably enhanced by the fact that the co-operatives have always aimed at putting good quality products at their members' disposal at reasonable prices.

The supply co-ops in our country have naturally been very much occupied with the question as to which feedstuffs could best be recommended to the farmer. Experience had shown in the meantime that the various types of animal required feedstuffs of diverse composition. A satisfactory answer to the question as to which feed would produce the best results could only be given, however, by combining scientific tests with practical experiments. To make this possible, the combined purchasing co-operatives in our country run an experimental farm, known as "de Schothorst", which farm has a well-equipped laboratory. The results obtained with various types of cattle, fed with mixed feeds composed by experts, has led to the increasing use of these feeds. The recipes for those feedstuffs, arrived at after a great deal of such experiment, are employed in the production of mixed feed in the supply co-ops' factories. The composition of the feed is always indicated on the label, and the co-operative factories have voluntarily submitted to the inspection of their production of this feed, carried out on behalf of the agricultural organisations.

For the rest, this farm is intended as a model farm. "De Schothorst" is a mixed farm, comprising an area of 150 acres, half of which is devoted to arable farming, part being used for livestock. The livestock comprises pigs and poultry as well as cattle. A problem is set in each section of the farm. A careful study is made not only of the results of the various methods of manuring and cultivating the soil and of the effect of various compositions of feedstuff on animals, but also of the arrangement of the livestock-stalls, sheds and other farm buildings, which is the subject of much experiment as well. The farm began with livestock of average quality, corresponding with that maintained by farmers in the immediate vicinity. Nowadays the farm has livestock of very high quality. "De Schothorst" is visited yearly by about 30,000 farmers, who are able to see with their own eyes the results it has been possible to achieve there. The farm receives no subsidy from the government.

chapter IV

Co-operatives for the marketing of agricultural produce *(marketing co-operatives)*

As the Dutch farmer began to produce more for the market and less for his own needs, the problem of the efficient marketing of his products became of greater urgency. As has already been remarked in chapter III, as a result of the decentralised character of Dutch farming, the farmer and market gardener are very often in an unfavourable position for bargaining with the buyers of their products. This is especially so when the products they have to offer are subject to deterioration or must be sold as soon as they are ready for the market, for instance, such products as vegetables, fruit, milk, pigs and eggs. The marketing co-operatives are accordingly of particular significance for such products. In the case of some products (e.g. milk and pigs) farmers dit not confine themselves to marketing but extended their activities to processing as well. These processing co-operatives are dealt with in chapter V.

Of the marketing co-operatives, the *horticultural auctions* occupy a special position. Before these auctions existed, the market gardener met with numerous difficulties in marketing his products. True enough, he could go and hawk his vegetables himself in a nearby centre of consumption or bring them to the local market there, but this method of selling involved the great disadvantage that unless he bought other products, he could not offer a wide enough assortment. Moreover, this method of marketing his products cost him a great deal of time, which could not be devoted to production. He could also sell his goods to the dealer, who visited his gardens to do business with him on the spot. In this case, however, the market gardener was usually in the weaker position for bargaining, since the dealer was generally better informed regarding the price trends of the products concerned. Moreover, if he felt he could not accept the dealer's offer, the market gardener had to wait until another dealer arrived.

Auctions were eventually set up more or less by chance, the first being established in 1887. An auction is a place where concentrated supply meets concentrated demand. The members of the auction deliver their products for sale in a large number of small lots, which are sold there to dealers regularly visiting the auction. For the dealers attendance at the auctions has the advantage that it saves them time, they formerly had to spend travelling from one market garden to another. There is sufficient competition among the dealers attending the auctions to assure the market gardeners getting a reasonable price for their produce.

Sale takes place by "Dutch auction", use being made of a clock, from which one can read off the prices. For every lot offered for sale these prices are shown successively by the hand of the clock in diminishing order, and as soon as a buyer thinks the price attractive, he presses a button next to his seat. The moment the hand of the clock stops, the number of the buyer's seat (each dealer has his own, permanent seat) is indicated on the clock. A note is taken of the price and the buyer's number, and the lot is sold. The auction takes place at very high speed. Sometimes 300 to 400 transactions are dealt with per clock per hour. Auctions often operate more than one clock at a time.

The selling is done by the auction, and the market gardener, who as a member of the auction brings his products along for sale, receives the money they yield from the auction cashier, after a certain percentage has been deducted to cover working costs. Sale takes place principally on the basis of cash down and only bona fide dealers are admitted to the auction.

The satisfactory operation of these auctions is mainly to be ascribed to the control the auction society exercises on the produce delivered for sale. The market gardeners are required to see that the lots offered for sale are, as far as possible, of uniform quality, which gives the dealer the assurance that the goods he is buying are all of the same quality. The sorting of produce according to quality is of great significance to the market gardener himself, for *the price* ultimately paid for the various lots brought to the market is *closely determined by quality,* and this acts as an important stimulus to the market gardener to pay great attention to raising the quality of his produce.

Although in the immediate vicinity of centres of consumption there are various auctions where retailers form the majority of buyers, in general, sale is made only to *wholesalers,* to exporters and to buyers from preserving factories. Actually, it is in the main the wholesalers who deal with home distribution and the export trade. The task of the auction does not extend beyond the sale of its members' products to the dealers. It provides the dealers with a convenient place for making large-scale purchases, a wide range of products being offered within a short period of time. More often than not the auction hall is situated alongside a railway or waterway and the dealer is able to rent some space on the premises for the despatch of the goods he has bought to his customers. The auction provides him with the necessary service in this respect. For instance, the exporter can make use of the packaging in which the market gardener brought the goods to the auction, such packaging being standardised as far as possible.

The most highly developed horticultural auctions are those for the sale of *vegetables and fruit;* there are also auctions for *cut flowers, potted plants,* etc. The latter are found in those districts where the cultivation of flowers forms an important section of horticulture, the co-operative flower auction at Aalsmeer, for instance, being world-famous.

The horticultural auctions in our country have become more and more important; practically every market gardener is a member of one. Their development has run parallel with the large-scale expansion that market gardening has undergone as a result of the growing opportunity to export products to the surrounding countries of Europe. With the rapid expansion of the home population sales in our own country have also increased considerably. As far as the soil permits, horticulture is pursued mainly in areas favourably situated for supplying home consumption markets or for the export trade. Although there are a number of very large auctions serving large production areas, in typical market gardening districts practically every village has its own auction.

There has been close co-operation between the almost 150 local auctions in existence [1]) since a central organisation was set up in 1918. This central organisation is the market gardeners' chief representative in the Netherlands. It has done much to raise the quality of horticultural produce; it organised a system of regular, collective advertisement to promote its sale; it has worked successfully for the introduction of uniform packaging; in short, its activities represent an important contribution towards strengthening the position of the auctions [2]).

---

[1]) Side by side with the co-operative horticultural auctions there are a few private auctions, which, although operating ostensibly according to the same system, naturally have a different aim, being run by private entrepreneurs.

[2]) As will be explained in further detail in chapter IX, to promote the smooth operation of a marketing co-operative, it is necessary in many cases to oblige the members to deliver produce to the auction. This is especially true of the Dutch horticultural auctions.

The Dutch market gardeners affiliated to a co-operative auction pursue their own policy, which aims as far as possible at securing a reasonable income for themselves, subject to the approval of the government, which, generally speaking, regards price-stabilisation as desirable. To this end, the auctions have jointly introduced a system of minimum prices. Produce which fails at the auction to secure the price, fixed beforehand by the auction authorities, is removed from the market, and another destination is sought for it, (e.g. it might be used as feedstuffs), which will not influence the normal demand. It should be mentioned that in such cases the minimum price is kept lower than the cost-price.

It is obvious that a marketing policy of this nature can only be effective, if all the horticultural produce is put on the market by one single organisation.

(Continued overleaf)

The auction system has not remained restricted to horticulture, but has also been successfully applied to *egg marketing*.

Up to about the year 1900, poultry farming was a more or less neglected sector of Dutch farming. Little attention was given to the stock of poultry, and the eggs were of very uneven size, weight and quality. The farmer's wife would sell these eggs either to buyers-up or to the local shopkeepers, and in both cases the price was often too low.

The egg auctions have brought about a considerable improvement in the farmers' position on the market. Not only have they created a market where adequate competition results in the products' fetching a reasonable price, but they have also graded the eggs according to quality and given the farmers advice on the better care of poultry, as a result of which egg production has been considerably improved. Nowadays, average production in our country is more than 200 eggs per hen per annum.

It is a remarkable fact that in the course of time most of the egg auctions have completely changed in character, developing into marketing societies, which themselves take charge of the sale of the eggs delivered by their members, and which even export large quantities of eggs to countries abroad. The egg auction pure and simple has practically disappeared, and nowadays the egg marketing co-operatives perform the same function as the great commercial houses. The largest of these co-operatives, established in the town of Roermond, has achieved a turnover of more than a million eggs a day. This organisation has set up a breeding station to raise the standard of poultry keeping. The egg co-operatives account for about 40 % of the total Netherlands export of this commodity.

Another animal product of which co-operative sales are of increasing significance is *wool*. From the beginning these co-operatives paid their members according to the quality of the wool delivered, and this made a great contribution to the improvement in quality of Dutch wool. On the other hand, the sale of the members' produce was stimu-

---

(Continued from page 31)

During the economic depression, when the funds required for pursuing this minimum price policy were provided by the government—nowadays the market gardeners provide these funds themselves—the government supported the policy by obliging market gardeners to sell their products via the auction, whether they were members or not. This measure has also been retained since the second world war. The effect of the obligation incumbent on market gardeners to use the auction has, however, recently been weakened by the fact that the producers are now allowed to sell outside the auction as well, though the transactions have to be reported to the auction. For this reason increasing propaganda is being carried on in auction circles to permit the auctions themselves to make regulations obliging members to sell their produce via the auction only.

lated by selling them articles, such as woollen thread and blankets, manufactured from wool. Recently a beginning has also been made with the industrial processing of wool delivered by members of the co-operative. Only one co-operative exists for this purpose. Its territory covers the entire country and it handles 90 % of all the wool produced by Dutch farmers.

Co-operatives have also been set up in our country for the organised sale of *slaughter-cattle*. This form of co-operative will be dealt with in further detail in chapter V, since it also has something of the nature of a processing co-operative.

The marketing of *milk*, insofar as the farmers market this product on a collective basis, takes place for the greater part via processing co-operatives, which will be discussed in chapter V. In the west of our country, however, where milk is used almost exclusively for human consumption in the large centres of population, there is a large marketing co-operative of recent origin, the Central Milk Co-operative. It was set up in 1944 and began its activities for the first time in 1945, after our country had been liberated from enemy occupation.

Although in earlier days, too, the farmers' bargaining position in this part of our country left much to be desired—that is, if they did not hawk their milk themselves—nevertheless the feeling of solidarity among these farmers was not sufficiently developed to allow of the setting up of a co-operative. The altered circumstances prevailing after the war have, however, finally convinced them that they can serve their own interests by working in a co-operative.

The Central Milk Co-operative now has a large number of members. The milk provided by its members is delivered via this organisation to the milk factories in the towns. Obviously, this concentrated supply helps to secure a better price for the milk, and by systematically paying for the milk delivered by the farmers according to quality, the quality has been improved, which improvement manifests itself in greater financial yields for the farmer.

Originally, the Central Milk Co-operative aimed exclusively at marketing its members' unprocessed milk, in order to strengthen its bargaining position on the market. In the mean time, however, it has begun to run a number of dairy factories and milk factories. All in all, it seems that a prosperous future awaits this co-operative.

As regards the co-operative marketing of *arable farming products,* this was limited in the beginning to seeds and seed potatoes. It is only in recent years that the co-operative marketing of grain crops has assumed any significance.

33

The most important factor in trading *seeds and seed potatoes* is that customers should be able to rely on the quality of these products. About the turn of the century, in order to be able to determine the quality of the seeds and seed potatoes they offered for sale, a group of cultivators decided to have the crops inspected while still in the field. Inspected crops were then marketed via the normal trade channels. When this scheme had proved unsatisfactory, the cultivators undertook the marketing themselves by setting up co-operatives for the purpose. In this way the customers of these co-operatives were always assured of good quality produce, while the cultivators were able to obtain a price in keeping with the quality of their wares.

Since 1932 the inspection of seeds and seed potatoes has been centralised in a national inspection service. Approved crops are sold through private channels as well as via the co-operatives.

The Netherlands carries on a large export trade in seeds and seed potatoes, partly to countries outside Europe. Both as regards the home market and the export trade the position occupied by the co-operatives in the marketing of seeds and seed potatoes is one of great significance. They handle 40 % of the home sale of seed potatoes, the corresponding figure for seeds being over 30 %. Their share in the export trade is estimated at the same figure.

The original demand for *grain marketing co-operatives* was not so strong. Grains are not subject to rapid deterioration, so that the farmer is able to store them himself, until such time as the market shows a favourable trend. Moreover, in those districts where production had from of old been destined for sale on the market, the market was well organised, so that price formation left little to be desired. It was when the cultivation of cereals for fodder, intended for sale on the market, became of significance in districts where the market for these crops was not yet well organised, that a need began to be felt for co-operative marketing. Since farmers often preferred to sell the grain fodder they themselves had cultivated and to buy mixed feeds in their place, the marketing of these fodder grains has become a task involving several purchasing co-operatives. Co-operative marketing, however, has now also been extended to the marketing of bread grains in districts where farmers formerly sold their crop themselves.

Another form of co-operative marketing is that performed by what are known as *dairy produce marketing societies,* operating on behalf of their affiliated co-operative dairy factories.

In the province of Friesland, where co-operative dairy farming has been of great importance from of old and where towards the end of the previous century there were already as many as eighty co-operative dairy factories, six of these factories decided to set up a separate organisation

34

for the sale of their products. The boards of these co-operative factories were of the opinion that co-operation ought not to cease with the joint management of a factory by the farmers, but that these co-operative dairy factories should in their turn co-operate to ensure that they did not compete with each other in marketing their products, which competition could have an unfavourable effect on the price of dairy produce. The central marketing organisation set up by these six co-operative dairy factories limited itself in the beginning to the marketing of butter, the affiliated factories agreeing to place a certain proportion of their butter production at its disposal. It was not long, however, before they were **agreeing to place their entire output of butter at the organisation's disposal.** They were prepared to do this because this method of marketing butter had met with good results. On the other hand, a general obligation to deliver all butter to the marketing organisation had proved necessary, because when the market was brisk, the affiliated factories had kept strictly to the requirement that obliged them to deliver only a portion of their production to the organisation, but as soon as they encountered any difficulty in getting rid of their product on the market, they had been inclined to offer the central organisation more than the compulsory quota.

As this central marketing organisation began to progress, more and more factories became affiliated. Later on the marketing of cheese was entrusted to it, and later still the marketing of other dairy products.

This development has inevitably led to strong influence being exercised by the marketing organisation over its affiliated factories. For it is the marketing organisation—and not its affiliated factories—which keeps closely in touch with the trend of the market and which is able to judge future sales opportunities. Thus, if sales-proceeds ar to be as high as possible, it will have to instruct the factories as regards the best range of products to put on the market. But naturally, if the central organisation is to influence production policy, it must bear the responsibility for the changes it introduces. Accordingly it pays the affiliated factories for the products they deliver to it a price, calculated to ensure that the members' gross milk proceeds remain the same, whatever variety of products the factory delivers to the marketing organisation. In determining this price, however, full account is taken of variations in quality in the products delivered by the different factories.

Similar marketing organisations for dairy produce have also been set up in other parts of our country, one of which restricts its activities to the marketing of butter. That cheese, too, which in a small area of our country is still manufactured on the farm, is marketed via one of these organisations, of which the farmers concerned are individual members. At the moment there is a total of seven dairy produce marketing organisations. Of the total number of co-operative dairy factories about 70 %

are affiliated to a marketing organisation. In 1956 these organisations, together with their affiliated factories handled — including the portion of their produce the latter marketed themselves — about $3/5$ of the total production of butter, over $2/5$ of the total production of cheese and almost $1/3$ of the total production of powdered milk.

Central marketing on behalf of affiliated co-operative factories is also met with in the potato-flour (farina) industry, further details of which follow in chapter V. Here, too, co-operation has remained limited to a proportion of the co-operative factories, though the proportion is considerably greater than in the case of the co-operative dairy produce industry, 13 of the 15 co-operative potato flour factories having joined the central marketing organisation.

Co-operatives for the processing of agricultural produce

A few examples will illustrate the success with which the co-operative movement in the Netherlands has met in the industrial field.

Of all the milk processed in our country in dairy and milk factories —and in view of the importance of the dairy-farming industry in the Netherlands that is a very large quantity—about 70 % is delivered to co-operatives. Of all the sugar produced in our country—and since our country is practically self-supporting as far as sugar is concerned this industry is of great importance too—about 66 % is manufactured in co-operative beet-sugar factories. Of the total production of strawboard —a typical Dutch product, the greater part of which is destined for the export market—65 % is provided by co-operative undertakings. Of the total output of farina—once again a typical Dutch export product— about 80 % is manufactured by co-operative factories. Of Dutch bacon —sold almost exclusively on the British market—the co-operatives supply almost the half. If one adds to these the co-operative manufacture of superphosphate, the co-operative flax industry and the co-operative meat processing, one obtains a good idea of the significance of the processing co-operatives in our country, even though this is not the whole story.

The setting up of the first co-operatives of this kind dates from the last years of the previous century and the first years of the present. The first co-operative dairy factory was established in 1886. In 1897 the first co-operative farina factory was founded and in 1899 the first co-operative strawboard factory. The first co-operative beet-sugar factory was established in the same year. A start was made with the co-operative processing of meat in 1916. In 1917 a co-operative super-phosphate factory was set up, and in 1920 a co-operative flax factory.

Up to about the year 1880 butter and cheese were made on the farms. This was the case all over the world. Certain technical inventions, however, made it more profitable to transfer the processing of milk from the farms to the factories. Private entrepreneurs took the initiative in setting up dairy factories, which bought the milk from the farmers in the surrounding district and turned it into dairy produce. The risks involved in processing the milk were thus borne by the private entrepreneurs.

Now, in the 'eighties of the previous century economic conditions in our country for farmers supplying milk were extremely bad, due in part to the economic depression reigning at the time. Accordingly, certain groups of farmers would have been only too happy if the dairy produce industry had developed more rapidly than was the case. They were of the opinion that a more modern form of milk processing might have a favourable influence on milk prices, and in the desperate situation in which they found themselves, any possibility of improvement was more than welcome. It is not surprising, therefore, that in these circumstances the farmers in a village in the north of our country, where dairy cattle-farming was the sole source of income, decided to work together on the building of a co-operative dairy factory for the manufacture of butter and cheese, after private enterprise had failed to found a dairy factory in the area and when negotiations with a local privately-owned factory had not led to the desired results. The fact that the founders of the factory were themselves skilled in the manufacture of butter and cheese facilitated the making of such a decision.

At about the same period, a form of co-operation between groups of farmers in the south of our country was also beginning to develop, their aim being to undertake the collective processing of milk into butter. Those concerned, all of them running small, mixed farms, produced only small quantities of milk. It was therefore only possible to found small factories, using manual labour, which required practically no capital investment and in which the members of the co-operative could actually perform the work with their own hands; at least to begin with.

When, in 1886, the *first co-operative dairy factory* was founded in the north of our country, the great problem facing its founders was how the new enterprise was to be financed. As will be explained in chapter X, this difficulty was met by laying down in the new co-operative society's statutes that its members bore unlimited liability for its financial commitments and that they were obliged, under all circumstances, to deliver the milk to this co-operative factory. Naturally, the secession of dissatisfied members was restricted by attaching certain conditions to this.

The first co-operative dairy factories were a success and were soon followed by others, so that at the present moment there are almost 400 of these factories in the Netherlands.

It follows from the above that as regards the establishment of the first co-operative dairy factories the initiative taken by the farmers supplying milk was of a supplementary character, since they proceeded to set up factories, run on their own account and at their own risk, in so far as private enterprise had in their opinion proved insufficient. Gradually, however, another element has come increasingly to the fore, that is to say, the element of competition with the private factories. This is to be explained by the fact that, in principle, the milk farmer's position in marketing his milk is a weak one. For milk is subject to deterioration and dairy farming, like agriculture in general, is decentralised in character. This means that the farmer must depend on a dairy factory not too far from his farm for disposing of his milk. He could, true enough, offer his product to a competing factory, but there were, and to a lesser extent still are, objections to the transport of milk over greater distances. Moreover, in the private sector of the dairy produce industry the local, privately-owned factories have tended increasingly to lose their independence, such factories having become part of one large concern, applying the same production policy, and therefore the same purchasing policy, everywhere, so that competition among the individual factories has completely disappeared. In these circumstances, it is clear that by running their own, i.e. co-operative, dairy factories, milk farmers have found an effective weapon for strengthening their position on the market. Accordingly, everywhere in the world where dairy cattle-farming is of any significance, co-operative dairy factories occupy an important position.

In addition to the fact that several factories are now run by one parent company, another form of concentration has manifested itself in the dairy produce industry in that the optimal capacity of the individual dairy factory has gradually increased. This is due, above all, to improved transport facilities, which have made it possible to convey the milk over greater distances. It is, however, also closely bound up with greater capital investment, which is a characteristic of the modern dairy-produce industry, in contrast to the small and primitive factories of the early days. The optimum capacity of the various types of dairy factory varies, particularly according to the type of machinery and installations used. It is smaller for a butter factory than for a butter and cheese factory, and much greater if condensed and powdered milk are also manufactured. In other words, the dairy industry is made up of factories which vary considerably in size. Although there is a trend towards amalgamation, as a result of the character of the raw material, milk, the industry will always be marked by a relatively high degree of decentralisation, compared with other branches of industry.

In running the first co-operative dairy factories, the problem arose as to the most reasonable method of *apportioning the net proceeds* among the members. Since the basic principle followed was that all members had the right to receive the same price for the same product, to begin with each member was naturally paid the same amount per gallon of milk. It soon became clear, however, that milk from one farm had a higher fat content than milk from another, so that such milk was of greater value for production purposes. Consequently payment was no longer made on the basis of quantity alone, but also on the basis of *quality*, i.e. fat content.

The application of this principle had important consequences. Determination of the fat content of milk delivered by various members soon led to the conclusion that differences of fat content per cow were greater than such differences per farm. Since the ability to produce milk of high fat content depends upon hereditary qualities, it was important to determine precisely what the production capacity of the various animals was. For, if for breeding purposes, only those animals were used which produced not only a large quantity of milk but also milk of high fat content, the milk yield per cow could be significantly increased.

On the instigation of the dairy produce co-operatives local milk control societies were accordingly set up, the aim of which was regularly to determine, by objective means, the milk yield per individual cow belonging to the members of the co-operative; that is to say, not only the amount of milk yielded but also, and particularly, its quality. In fact these milk control societies can be regarded as extensions of the co-operative dairy factories, though membership is not always identical.

Particulars as to fat content recorded by these milk control societies are assembled by the herd books, whereby the information is made available to those purchasing cattle for breeding purposes. Later on, groups of cattle farmers delivering their milk to privately-owned dairy factories set up their own milk control societies, so that this difference between co-operative and non-co-operative dairy factories has gradually fallen into the background. Nevertheless, the stimulus given by the co-operatives to improve the cattle herd was of great importance and, indeed, still is. To avoid any misunderstanding it should be remarked that in determining differences in quality, which forms the basis of the prices paid to members of co-operatives for the milk they deliver, the fat content is no longer the only criterion employed. In this respect as well the dairy produce co-operatives have done pioneer work.

These co-operatives have also devoted their attention to the systematic combating of contagious diseases among cattle. Here, too, there has been close co-operation between the co-operative dairy produce organisations and the herd books.

The *co-operative potato-flour (farina) industry* is a typical Dutch industry. That is to say, in a certain aera of our country potatoes are cultivated in large quantities exclusively for the purpose of manufacture, these potatoes being less suitable for human consumption.

The first farina factory in the Netherlands dates from about the year 1840. The industry gradually expanded, so that by the end of the

Supply co-ops are active
in the field of
seed-improvement

The Dutch auction
has served as a model
for other countries

In horticultural districts the Dutch canals are used for transporting vegetables to the auction

A regional organisation for marketing dairy-produce

previous century it occupied a position of importance. The stimulus to found a co-operative farina industry lay in the fact that, in 1897, various farina factories formed a union which fixed uniform buying prices for its member factories. By so doing, private industry caused resistance to grow amongst the suppliers of the raw material, who were entirely dependent upon these factories for the sale of their products. Since economic conditions during the preceding twenty years had already been exceptionally bad, and since the founding of co-operative dairy factories had proved a success, in 1897 a group of farmers cultivating potatoes for manufacture decided to set up a co-operative for the manufacture of farina from their potatoes.

Generally speaking, the potato farmers had better capital resources than had the cattle farmers who joined the first co-operative dairy factories. Moreover, they wanted to make themselves as independent as possible of third parties. Accordingly, whereas the memorandum of association contained the principle of unlimited liability, each member had in addition to take at least one share of 500 guilders in the co-operative, which share involved the obligation to deliver a certain quantity of potatoes to the factory every year.

Despite early disappointments, the success of the first co-operative in this field was soon assured and by 1914 there were already 20 co-operative farina factories in our country, together processing $2/3$ of all manufacturing potatoes produced. At the present time there are 15 co-operative farina factories and the share of the private sector of this industry has been reduced to about 20 %. It should, however, be noted that the private sector concerns itself to a far greater degree than does the co-operative sector with the further processing of farina into other products.

The *co-operative strawboard factories* represent another typical branch of co-operative production in the Netherlands. In the same district where potatoes are cultivated for industrial purposes, conditions are particularly favourable for straw-processing. There is a large amount of straw per acre of cultivated land, and thanks to a close network of canals in this area, the cost of transporting this straw, for which the marketing possibilities are limited, is low.

About the turn of the century there were 10 strawboard factories in this region of our country and the general impression was that they were making handsome profits. This was a source of annoyance to the suppliers of the straw, and although straw is a relatively unimportant product in the farming industry, they asked themselves whether they could not secure a better bargaining position by undertaking the manufacture of strawboard themselves.

One difficulty with which the farmers were confronted was that they were entirely ignorant of the production process; moreover, the trade in this product—mainly export to Great Britain—was shrouded in mystery, which would not make it easy for a new factory to secure an entry into the market. Nevertheless, in 1899 a group of farmers decided to set up a co-operative strawboard factory. The capital required amounted to about 10 times the capital required for the first farina factory on co-operative lines and about 15 times as much as was required to set up the first co-operative dairy factory.

The principle of members' unlimited liability was accepted in founding this co-operative too. Moreover, members accepted the obligation to take at least one share of 1000 guilders, to be paid up at once, which share also obliged them to supply the factory with a given quantity of straw, whatever the circumstances. All the same, it was a fairly difficult business to secure the necessary loans, the share capital representing only a fraction of the total capital required for the project. Accordingly members were further required to stand guarantee for the payment of the interest on, and the redemption of, the debenture loan that the co-operative eventually succeeded in raising.

Nowadays there are 19 strawboard factories in our country, of which 10 are on a co-operative basis and 9 private enterprises.

Strawboard is a remarkable article. It is used for packaging and the main market for it is in Great Britain. The demand for strawboard is relatively inelastic, which means that high prices for it cause only a slight decrease in the demand, as long as such prices remain below the level of other articles that can be used as a substitute for strawboard, such, for instance, as packaging materials manufactured from wood, which form the main substitute. On the other hand a reduction in the price does not automatically bring about an increase in the demand for strawboard, this being determined exclusively by the turnover of goods requiring to be packed.

In these circumstances the joint producers of strawboard can obtain a good price for their product by limiting the total quantity offered for sale on the British market. This has been the reason for the close co-operation existing between the co-operative and the privately-run strawboard factories in our country. The success of their joint action is to be ascribed to the circumstance that the Netherlands is practically the sole producer of strawboard and the number of factories producing it is small.

The limitation of the amount put on the market, however, involves a restriction on production and this in turn leads to the fixing of production quotas per factory. But the fixing of such a maximum means that the joint members of a co-operative factory may not exceed such a maximum either. This soon leads to a limitation of membership. Although the co-operative strawboard factories have not expressly rejected the principle that membership should be open to all, in practice the admission of new members is restrained by the fact that membership is only possible by purchasing one or more shares, the prices of which often undergo great fluctuations, depending on the state of the market. Thus, when in the years immediately preceding the last world war, conditions were favourable for the strawboard industry and the co-operative factories permitted the adherence of new members on an insufficient scale, a number of farmers who were not members asked themselves whether they ought not to set up a new co-operative factory. The war prevented the execution of this plan, and when the war was over the ground for proceeding with it had disappeared, since straw now commanded high prices, even if it was not processed into strawboard; furthermore, import restrictions in Great Britain have had an unfavourable effect on the demand.

Sugar beets for industrial processing were being cultivated in the Netherlands as early as the middle of the previous century. The factories were run by private entrepreneurs. Towards the end of the century, these entrepreneurs signed an agreement enabling them to bring great influence to bear on the conditions for delivering sugar beets to the various factories. This, together with complaints which the producers of sugar beets had been harbouring for some years, was the reason why, in 1892, a group of farmers attempted to set up a co-operative factory.

This first attempt did not lead to the desired result. When, however, in 1897, the private manufacturers, convinced that the farmers would not build a factory of their own, made the conditions for the delivery of sugar beets still more onerous, the desire to set up co-operative factories received a further powerful stimulus.

The *first co-operative beet sugar factory* in our country was established in 1899. In founding it, the farmers had taken on a task of considerable dimensions. In contrast to the situation in the dairy industry, they knew as little about the production process as the founders of the first co-operative strawboard factory had known about the production process for strawboard. Moreover, the founding of a sugar factory required far more capital than any other form of processing the co-operative movement had so far undertaken. For reasons which will be set out in more detail in the chapter dealing with financing (chapter X), the introduction of the principle of unlimited liability met with difficulty. Accordingly the co-operative sugar factory was financed on the basis of shares involving limited liability only, coupled, however, with an obligation to deliver a certain quantity of beets to the new factory.

Although it seemed at first that the founding of a co-operative sugar factory would also lead to success, very serious difficulties were encountered later on, and it was touch and go whether the factory would not have to go into liquidation. This was avoided, however, by the fact that the members of the board came forward as guarantors, placing the whole of their capital at the co-operative's disposal for this purpose. This gesture restored the confidence of those who had invested loans in the co-operative, which now had an opportunity to show what is was worth. All the same, this experience had an unfavourable influence on other farmers contemplating the setting up of further co-operative sugar factories, and it was not until 1909 that a second such factory was established. Hereafter, however, five more followed fairly soon, the last of these being founded in 1914. It cost almost 3 million guilders.

At the time the first co-operative sugar factory was set up, there were about thirty privately-owned factories in our country. Once the co-operative factories had got over their growing pains and had developed into large-scale undertakings, most of the private factories proved unable to compete with their more modern and larger co-operative rivals. The private sector of the industry then resorted to concentration in order to be able to maintain its position. A number of factories were closed down by mutual agreement, while the rest placed themselves under one management. At the moment there remain six privately-owned factories manufacturing beet sugar; these form part of a parent company and consequently apply the same policy. There are also six co-operative factories, of which three have been closely co-operating for some years now, as a result of which their position has been considerably strengthened.

The co-operative factories include two with a capacity for processing about 7000 tons of beets every twenty-four hours, from which they produce about 1000 tons of white sugar. These are the largest beet sugar factories in the world.

The great size of the beet sugar factories in our country is due primarily to the fact that a close network of canals makes it possible to transport beets cheaply, even over great distances. Moreover, in view of the obligation members have to deliver a certain quantity of beets to the factory, as more shares are placed, a co-operative factory can reckon on a corresponding increase in the supply of beets, which considerably facilitates any decision to increase working capacity. All the private factories can do, however, is to conclude agreements every year with the suppliers of beets. At the present moment the six co-operative factories in our country process more than 60 % of the beets cultivated.

Co-operative manufacture has been applied in the field of *flax-processing* too, likewise with the aim of strengthening the farmer's bargaining position on the market.

There have from of old been several possibilities open to the cultivator of flax for marketing his product. He could sell his flax in its raw condition to dealers, who made large-scale purchases on behalf of the

44

processing industry; he could also sell it to the local manufacturer, who processed it in a simply-equipped workshop and then sold it to the trade in the form of flax tow. Finally, the farmer could produce the flax tow himself by having his labourers undertake the processing operation as a 'cottage industry' during the winter months. This last method relieved seasonal unemployment in agriculture at a time when no system of unemployment relief was in force.

But although there were several avenues open to the farmer for marketing his product, this did not mean that he could always obtain a reasonable price for his flax. As in the case of other agricultural products, his position in negotiations with wholesalers was a weak one. Nor did the processing of the flax before it was sold bring in more money, for the finished product was not of a very high standard. The processing was done almost entirely by hand and this lack of mechanisation meant that the finished product was of unequal quality.

After the first world war the unsatisfactory position as regards the price obtained for flax was further accentuated by the fact that the demand from Belgium declined. The Belgian manufacturing industry had always taken a large quantity of unprocessed flax from the Dutch farmers, but owing to the destruction of part of its industrial capacity, it now bought a small quantity only. The fact, however, that processed flax was fetching good prices, caused a group of farmers in the south west of our country to decide, in 1920, to establish a co-operative factory for flax manufacture, whereby they would be able to apply modern methods of production.

Although the enterprise had to fight against great disappointments in the early stages — on several occasions the factory suffered damage from fire—this co-operative has met with success, particularly since the second world war. The decisive factor leading to this success was the persever- ance of a number of its leading figures, and of its chairman in particular.

In this industry, the flax supplied by the members of the co-operative is processed into flax tow, employed in the textile industry, and into linseed, which, insofar as it is not exported as seed for sowing, is used by Dutch manufacturers of linseed oil. The co-operative factory is assured of a regular supply of the raw material since, coupled with the possession of a share in the co-operative—and every member is obliged to take at least one share—is an obligation to deliver a certain quantity of flax.

The co-operative flax factory is the only large concern in the Nether- lands working in the field of flax manufacture. A few years ago it extended its activities by building a spinning mill.

The intensive nature of livestock farming in the Netherlands is mani- fested, inter alia, by the great importance of the pig-keeping sector. Pigs are processed into fresh meat, bacon and preserved meat. All three finished products are destined partly for export, the bacon being almost exclusively for this purpose.

A large number of privately-operated exporting slaughter-houses had devoted themselves from of old to the export of fresh meat, particularly to the English market. When, in the middle 'twenties, the export of fresh meat to England was prohibited, the manufacture of bacon assumed great importance. Since this industry required a greater concentration of capital, it was principally the big concerns that were successful in this branch. The same applies to the canned meat industry, which also grew in importance. As a result of the consequent tendency to concentration, the farmer's marketing position, which was no stronger in marketing his pigs than it was in marketing his other products, was further undermined.

Even before the first world war attemps were made to set up *co-operative slaughter-houses,* but no permanent results were achieved. Finally, under the pressure of circumstances, a number of co-operative slaughter-houses were set up during the inter-war period and these managed to secure for themselves a modest share of the bacon industry. Gradually, however, two large private concerns operating in the bacon industry became more and more powerful as time went on, and this gave rise to a certain unrest among farmers, since they feared that these concerns would eventually be able to dictate the price paid for pigs. This uneasiness led to greater co-operation among the existing co-operatives. A part of them united to form a central organisation, which embraced co-operative factories, hitherto independent. Since these factories are now being run as a unit, the co-operative movement's competitive power in the meat-processing sector has been appreciably strengthened.

At present the particular task of the regional co-operatives affiliated to this central organisation is to supply the factories with the required supply of livestock, mainly pigs. For the rest, they also attend to the marketing of their members' livestock, insofar as this is not delivered for processing in the co-operative factories.

As was already said in chapter III, the organisation of co-operative societies in the Netherlands is characterised by groupings originating from different beliefs and philosophies of life. These differences also affect the organisation of the co-operatives in this field. Thus a number of cattle-marketing and meat-processing co-operatives have not joined the above-mentioned central organisation but have formed a separate federation, operating mainly in the south of our country.

Concentration in the co-operative meat-processing sector has greatly benefited the co-operatives in this field. At the present time the co-operatives handle almost half the total production of bacon in the Netherlands. The co-operatives have also made good progress in recent years in the manufacture of preserved (canned) meat.

46

In this chapter on processing co-operatives we would also mention a co-operative undertaking that, though not actually concerned with the processing of agricultural produce, nevertheless occupies an important position in the ranks of agricultural co-operatives, since it supplies the farmers with an industrial product of growing significance, that is to say, artificial fertilizer.

The use of fertilizers, expressed as a figure per acre, is higher in the Netherlands than anywhere else in the world. Generally speaking, the powerful development of their supply co-ops enabled the farmers to obtain fertilizer at reasonable prices. This was, however, hardly the case with superphosphate. Production of superphosphate used to be highly concentrated in the Netherlands, as a result of which the product was only obtainable at a high price. Consequently, in 1917, arable farmers from various parts of our country determined upon the establishment of a co-operative factory for the manufacture of superphosphate. The sulphuric acid required for the preparation of this fertilizer was originally purchased from outside, but later on the co-operative went over to establishing its own sulphuric acid factory. More recently it has also taken to producing its own phosphorous acid.

This *co-operative fertilizer factory* has grown into a large enterprise. The raw material has to be imported, the main source of supply being North Africa. Since sales in this industry are markedly seasonal in character—in the Netherlands, for instance, the use of fertilizer is confined principally to the spring and autumn—and since, moreover, superphosphate cannot be kept for a long time, it has proved necessary to extend the market to the southern hemisphere. This was necessary to make the industry pay, for it requires the investment of considerable capital.

The Dutch co-operative fertilizer factory has been able to extend its sales in South Africa, in particular. Originally the superphosphate was shipped to this market in sacks, but it soon proved more economical to ship it in bulk and to pack it on arrival. This has led to the establishment of a subsidiary concern in South Africa, which is now also concerned with production. Naturally, as a result of this development, sales of fertilizer to members of the co-operative form only a limited percentage of the total turnover.

The setting up of this artificial fertilizer factory involved great risks. Accordingly, as in the case of other processing co-operatives, use was made of shares. In this way the risk involved for the members was limited, while the co-operative superphosphate factories were assured of selling a certain minimum quantity of fertilizer, for each share carries with it an obligation to take a certain quantity of superphosphate from the factory every year, whatever the circumstances. As the co-operative has proved a great success, the possession of a share is now regarded as a

47

privilege, giving one the right to obtain fertilizer at cost-price, rather than as an obligation.

The First Netherlands Co-operative Fertilizer Factory produces about one third of all the superphosphate manufactured in the Netherlands.

chapter VI

Consumers' co-operatives

As has appeared from the foregoing chapters, the agricultural co-operative originated more often than not from a desire on the part of farmers to improve their social and economic position within the existing framework of society. The history of the consumers' co-operative is also intimately bound up with that of an economically weak group, namely the industrial workers.

The first consumers' co-operative society originated in England as a reaction to the abuses resulting from the industrial revolution, that came about in that country at the beginning of the 19th century. This industrial revolution had caused the workers to become highly dependent upon the employers and particularly in the first phase of this new development they were obliged to be content with an extremely low standard of living. Moreover, as a result of periodic unemployment, the workers were at the disadvantage of usually having to buy the necessities of life from those shopkeepers who were willing to grant them credit. Furthermore, since many employers were also the shopkeepers, the truck system was often introduced, so that the workers were still more dependent upon them. Finally, consumers in general had in those days much cause for complaint: besides having to pay very high prices for their food, they often got short weight into the bargain, while the quality of the goods was as often as not far from being all that could be desired.

A first successful attempt to bring about an improvement in this state of affairs was made in 1844 by 28 weavers of Rochdale, who set up a consumers' co-operative society. The aim of the *Rochdale Society of Equitable Pioneers* was far wider, however. Besides their desire to serve the direct interests of the members, the founders of this co-operative society also aimed, according to an express provision in their statutes, "to arrange the powers of production, distribution, education and government, or, in other words, to establish a selfsupporting home colony of united interests or assist other societies in establishing such colonies". That is, their ideal was to bring about a fundamental reform in the organisation of society which would result in a more equitable distribution of the national income. The interests of the

49

consumer would hereby be given priority, in the sense that production would not be a mere result of business activity but be directly aimed at satisfying the needs of society.

It was in conformity with the aims of the Rochdale Pioneers that membership of the co-operative society should be open to all. In other words, everyone who sympathised with the society's aims and was prepared to abide by its rules, could become a member.

The other *principles* of the first consumers' co-operative were:

a) democratic organisation, which implied not only that every member had one vote, but particularly that the supreme authority in the society resided in the general meeting, which chose the board, which board had to report every year to the general meeting of members on its management of the society's affairs;

b) the goods purchased jointly were put at the disposal of members for cash payment and at prevailing market prices;

c) surpluses not used to augment the society's working capital were to be apportioned among the members on the basis of the amount each member had spent;

d) interest was to be paid at a fixed percentage on the capital members subscribed.

The principles adopted by this first consumers' co-operative proved their utility in practice and the principles laid out above form the basis of consumers' co-operatives to this day. Today as well the primary aim of these co-operative societies is to serve the interest of the consumer. On the other hand, the aim to reform the existing social order gradually disappeared from the rules of such societies. We cannot go into the reasons for this here. Suffice it to say that the labour movement —with which the first consumers' co-operatives were intimately connected—gradually changed in character. Generally speaking, as it appeared that an appreciable improvement could be brought about in the position of the workers within the existing framework of society, the aim of the labour movement to bring about a reorganisation of the social order lost most of its force. This also explains why in most countries the consumers' co-operative society has taken on a more general character, a conscious attempt having been made to extend membership to other groups of consumers besides the workers.

The enterprise of the Rochdale Pioneers proved a great success, which was due to the economical way in which this first consumers' co-operative functioned. In the beginning the cost of running the society was, in fact, practically nil: the goods bought were made available to the members at the secretary's private address during certain hours of the evening. Since they were sold at the market price and not at the cost price, growing surpluses were built up every year, and the small capital the members had managed to scrape together gradually increased as a consequence. This made it possible in turn to increase the society's turnover, while at the same time the number of members grew.

The example the Rochdale Pioneers had set was followed on a grand scale, so that there were soon numerous local consumers' societies in the United Kingdom. After a time these societies proceeded to found *central organisations*. These central bodies—two were founded in Great Britain, one for England and Wales and one for Scotland—functioned as central purchasing organisations on behalf of the local societies and helped in their turn to reinforce the position of these local co-operatives. The activity of these wholesale societies did not, however, remain limited to buying; they also turned their hand to production.

Thus it was that co-operative factories were established for the manufacture of biscuits, soap, shoes, flour, tobacco, margarine, cotton goods, etc. In addition, the consumers' co-operative entered the field of insurance, while co-operative sickness funds were also founded under its auspices. At the present day the consumers' co-operative societies in the United Kingdom are also active in banking; they even run hotels.

A similar development of the consumers' co-operative society can also be witnessed in other countries, in Scandinavia, Switzerland and Germany in particular.

In the *Netherlands* it was not until 1876 that the *first consumers' co-operative* was set up, although numerous attempts had been made before that date to imitate the example set by the Rochdale Pioneers. Remarkable enough, it was primarily intellectuals, well disposed towards the workers, who made much propaganda for the consumers' co-operative, though this propaganda did not lead to the desired result. It was not only that the workers were rather suspicious of suggestions made by others on their behalf; one of the main obstacles was their desire to obtain immediate financial benefits from the consumers' co-operatives, so that they failed to take sufficient account of the need to consolidate their financial position first of all.

Moreover, the first consumers' co-operative in the Netherlands, which was named "Eigen Hulp" (Self-Help) and established in the Hague, was of a remarkable character. For at its foundation membership was confined to brain workers, manual workers being deliberately excluded. The aim of "Eigen Hulp" was accordingly far more to help to raise the purchasing power of its members by running co-operative shops, than to bring about reorganisation of society, which at the time was the aim of practically all those concerned with the consumers' co-operative. Although "Eigen Hulp" worked on the lines of the Rochdale Society, except as regards membership, the founders of this co-operative society were, in fact, inspired by the example of the Austrian Unions of civil servants rather than by the Rochdale Pioneers. But this type

51

of "civil servants co-operative society" remained confined to this single case. Later on, moreover, "Eigen Hulp" also adopted the principle of making membership open to all.

It goes without saying that the workers' reaction to the setting up of a consumers' co-operative society that excluded them from membership was to set up co-operatives of their own. This they did not only in the Hague but elsewhere in our country as well. Such co-operatives were very often regarded as a part of the trades union movement. Accordingly, their statutes often contained a clause to the effect that a portion of the surpluses formed had to be put at the disposal of the trades union. This hampered the development of the consumers' co-operative, since consumers less friendly inclined towards the trades unions were consequently less inclined to become members [1]).

As a result of the fact that in our country the labour movement has also been organised on the basis of belief and philosophy of life, three kinds of consumers' co-operatives, in addition to the "Eigen Hulp" type, came into being. These were the so-called general consumers' co-operatives that in reality were socialist in character, consumers' co-operatives that in actual fact were confined to Roman Catholic workers, and a group of consumers' co-operatives of Protestant character. Of these the first group was the most important.

In 1889, under the influence of "Eigen Hulp", a form of *collaboration* had already come about among the various kinds of local co-operatives, and "Eigen Hulp" exercised a great influence over this national union. The union declined in significance when the various groups of workers' co-operatives began, one after the other, to unite in non-commercial central organisations of their own. The local co-operatives, however, continued to be members of the special joint purchase section of the above-mentioned national union. Once this section was turned into an independent organisation, it was able to develop into a true national wholesale co-operative society. This central purchasing organisation of the consumers' co-operatives in the Netherlands has progressed favourably. It did, it is true, suffer considerable losses immediately after the first world war, but the difficulties it encountered were soon overcome, thanks partly to a government loan, which was later repaid in full.

A significant change came about in the organisation of the consumers' co-operatives in this country, when, a few years after the second world

---

[1]) It may be mentioned that association with the labour movement is also characteristic of the consumers' co-operatives in Belgium and France. Consumers' co-operatives in Scandinavia, on the other hand, have been of a general character from their very beginnings. The first consumers' co-operatives in Denmark were rural co-operatives, which embraced practically the entire population of the village.

war, the non-commercial unions of the three groups of workers' co-operative societies were dissolved, being amalgamated with the national wholesale society to form the *Central Society of Netherlands Consumers' Co-operatives,* which has since developed into a financially powerful body.

The number of local co-operative societies in the Netherlands is now about 275, comprising 390,000 members. As a rule only the head of the family is a member, so that, putting the average family at 4, it may be taken that about 14 % of the population of the country support the consumers' co-operatives. Of the 275 local societies, 267, with over 340,000 members, are affiliated to the Central Society of Netherlands Consumers' Co-operatives. Together they run about 1250 shops. In general, the consumers' co-operatives in the Netherlands are supported principally by the organised workers, this as a result of their history. As a consequence, their shops are found chiefly in the large centres of population. However, in wide areas of our country the movement is gathering force in rural districts as well. It sometimes happens that a consumers' co-operative is combined with an agricultural purchasing co-operative (supply co-op), though this is highly exceptional.

The local co-operative societies trade in the main in groceries and allied products, these representing about 50 % of their joint total turnover; the share of bread and pastry comes to approximately 25 %. Most of the local consumers' co-operatives of any size run their own bakery. Fuel is also important, and the members can also buy textiles, household articles, shoes, tobacco and cigarettes. Three consumers' co-operatives run dairies, one of these being of large size, and a few others also run butchers' shops. A co-operative laundry exists in the Hague, in which town there is also a large co-operative sickness benefit fund with its own hospital and maternity home. This fund originated from the consumers' co-operative and is closely allied with it, the management of both organisations being in the same hands.

The Central Society of Netherlands Consumers' Co-operatives, mentioned above, which is the national buying agency and of which practically all the local consumers' co-operatives are members, has not limited its activities to the purchase of goods on behalf of its member co-operative societies. It has also successfully undertaken its own *production* and nowadays runs factories in various parts of our country. In Rotterdam it has two flour mills, a coffee factory and a tea-packing factory, and in Utrecht, a central factory where soap, edible oils and fats, cake, rusks, biscuits, vermicelli and other flour products, cocoa, chocolate and sugar confectionery, jams and lemonade, polish and cosmetics are manufactured. In other places there are factories producing textiles, tobacco and cigars. The Society also has its own cheese storehouse. Its headquarter offices are situated at Rotterdam, while it has two branch offices, one in the east and the other in the south of our country. As in the other countries, too, the consumers' co-operative movement in the Netherlands also operates with success in the field of mutual insurance.

The local consumers' co-operatives are not obliged to purchase all the products the Central Society deals in from the Society, though naturally they agree to do so, in principle, when joining the organisation. For the local co-operative societies do not lose their autonomy even though by accepting membership of the Central Society, they assume of course the obligations attached to such acceptance. In actual fact, they do take what goods they can from the Central Society, though "co-operative loyalty" is greater in the case of the one local co-op than in the case of the other. Account is taken of the degree of loyalty shown in distributing the surpluses of the Central Society among members.

Summing up, it can be said that the development of the consumers' co-operative movement in the Netherlands has been influenced by the more or less chance circumstance that membership of the first local consumers' co-operative was barred to precisely that group of consumers which, taking the consumers' co operative movement as a whole, now form the majority of its members. This led to the setting up of consumers' co-operatives whose customers are principally the organised workers.

In comparison with other countries, the scope of the consumers' co-operative movement in our country is limited. Yet it is a factor of significance and in many respects its organisation can be said to be powerful.

chapter VII

Other forms of co-operative

Attention will be paid in this chapter to a number of other forms of co-operatives that have grown up in our country. Those concerned are co-operative societies providing certain services, co-operative societies working in the field of insurance and retail traders' co-operatives.

The *co-operatives which provide services* (service co-ops) are of great variety.

In the field of *services to private individuals,* mutual burial funds and funeral service societies are in existence and are of significance not only in rural areas but in a number of towns as well. The co-operative exploitation of locker plants for household purposes, which in many countries has gradually assumed significant proportions, was recently introduced in the Netherlands and is undergoing favourable development.

As regards *services to farmers covering certain farming operations,* here, too, we find a variety of specialised co-operatives. In our country there are a great number of co-operative societies which provide storehouses for seed potatoes. The storage of seed potatoes sets high requirements as regards the temperature and degree of humidity of the surrounding atmosphere, requirements it is difficult for the individual farmer to meet. Collaboration between farmers also takes the form of co-operative grass drying-houses. Also worthy of mention are co-operatives which promote the cultivation of medicinal and aromatic herbs and their drying.

More significant is the provision of services by *co-operatives for the use of agricultural machinery.* In our country, where in many regions the small farm predominates, the individual farmers cannot make the use of agricultural machinery pay its way. As a result of this, hiring agencies have acquired great importance. These are enterprises which own various kinds of agricultural machines and have trained personnel to use the machines at their disposal. For a certain sum of money they lend the farmers their services for the performance of a large variety of activities, such as tillage, threshing of the harvest and so on.

Even before the second world war agricultural machinery was being used on a co-operative basis to enable farmers to enjoy a share in the benefits of mechanisation. Some supply co-ops acquired machines in order to hire them out to their members. Before the war, moreover, a considerable number of threshing societies for the joint use of threshing machinery were already in existence.

When, after the war, mechanisation made great strides in agriculture, the number of machines used in farming rapidly increased. It was not only a question of replacing draught animals by tractors; machines also began to be employed for other purposes too. Mention can be made of harvesting combines, various kinds of sowing machines, fertilizer spreaders, spraying and harvesting machines. A need to extend the joint use of agricultural machinery arose among small farmers, who could not employ them economically, working on their own, and an increasing number of co-operatives were set up for the purpose. In its endeavour to stimulate a rationalised system of farming, especially on the smaller farms, in order to keep down the cost-price of agricultural products, the government has greatly encouraged the joint use of agricultural machinery since the war. The specialised agricultural machinery co-operatives have benefited particularly from its aid, the government having until recently granted them subsidies. In view of the interest the smaller farms have in these co-operative societies, such subsidies increased in amount as the number of small farms affiliated to those co-operatives rose. Subsidies were not granted to departments of other types of co-operative (e.g. supply co-ops) which also hire out agricultural machines to their members. The effect of these measures has been a large increase in the number of agricultural machinery co-operatives in our country during the post-war period. Time must show whether this type of co-operative will prosper even without government aid.

This form of co-operation is not easy. When threshing machines had been used on a joint basis by the threshing societies set up at an earlier date, little difficulty had been encountered in framing a roster for use of machines by the members, threshing being a process which can be spread out over a fairly long period of time. But in the case of work in the field, the time at which most operations must be performed is determined by the seasons, weather conditions and by the natural course of the production process, harvesting operations, for instance, being tied to a strict time-table. This means that the farmers belonging to an agricultural machinery co-operative often need to use some machine or other at the same time. Consequently, for such a co-operative to be able to operate successfully, not only is good management needed but a good deal of mutual understanding and a real will to co-operate. For this reason it is advisable to keep the operational area of such co-operatives as small as possible; the better the members know each other, the more accommodating they are likely to be among themselves. On the other hand, certain machines can only be run economically, even by a co-operative society,

At this marketing co-op
a million eggs are inspected
and graded every day

85 % of Dutch cheese
is made in co-operative
factories

Modern equipment is an essential condition for the manufacture of high quality dairy produce

The largest sugarfactories in Europe are run by farmers

if they are employed over large acreages. Moreover, only large co-operative societies are in a position to maintain a reserve of machines and keep a repair shop going. In our country the disadvantages associated with small co-operatives are removed by two or three or more co-operatives working together and using on a collective basis a workshop, reserve machines and machines it is not economical for a co-operative to run, working on its own.

Most agricultural machinery co-operatives only hire out machines that their members can operate themselves; others supply tractors and other machines which require more expert knowledge for their employment. The latter usually employ a permanent staff of operators, who are placed at the farmers' disposal with the machines. The rates charged by agricultural machinery co-operatives are usually based on the length of time the machines are put at their members' disposal. In order to secure the most intensive use of the machinery available, this method is better than charging a rate per unit of acreage.

Artificial insemination co-operatives represent a group of service co-ops which have been set up in our country only since the war. These are co-operative societies which possess one or more bulls used for the artificial insemination of cows belonging to the member farmers. The primary aim of these co-operative societies is to improve the standard of the cattle herd by using superior animals for breeding purposes. Artificial insemination is, moreover, a succesful way of combating certain contagious diseases among cattle. As better results are naturally obtained when superior quality bulls are used, and as one bull can be used for the insemination of a large number of cows, it is advisable that the artificial insemination co-operatives should operate over a reasonably wide field, for it is easier for a large society than for a small one to purchase bulls at a high price and make them pay.

Artificial insemination has made great progress in our country. Whereas in 1949 only 12 % of all cows were artificially inseminated, this percentage has now risen to about 55. Although this form of co-operation was originally intended to enable small farmers to make use of good breeding material, artificial insemination is being increasingly adopted by the large farmers. Livestock farmers principally concerned with marketing breeding cattle show little interest in these co-operatives.

In some parts of our country the artificial insemination co-operatives originated from bull farms or breeding societies; in other areas great encouragement to set them up was forthcoming from the co-operative dairy factories, some of which began to operate their own artificial insemination stations. Purchasing co-operatives (supply co-ops) have also made their contribution. Nowadays the great majority of co-operatives for artificial insemination are independent societies.

Another form of service which can be mentioned in this context is that provided by societies running *agricultural accounting bureaux*. Such bureaux charge themselves with the bookkeeping on behalf of their members. Originally, the primary aim of these societies was to assist their members on taxation questions. But there has been a growing endeavour to make use of the bookkeeping particulars in managing the farm. This work must be regarded as of great importance, for it is only by means of reliable bookkeeping that one can ascertain whether a farm is being run on an economic basis.

The application of the co-operative idea in the field of insurance has led to the development of various *mutual insurance societies.*

There is some confusion in practice as regards the term "mutual". A mutual insurance society is an assurance enterprise which is run by, and for the account of, the members. The insured, as a collective body, represent the highest authority in the society and they choose the board, which is responsible for supplying the general meeting with a report on the conduct of the society's business at regular intervals. A second characteristic of mutual insurance societies is that loss and damage suffered is borne jointly by the insured, which in practice means a variable premium each year. Now, there exists a group of insurance societies which apply the principle of the variable premium in contrast to fixed premiums— insofar as a part of the premium paid is returned to the insured, if the profit made justifies this. On these grounds such societies also claim to be mutual insurance societies. But it must be remarked in this connection that there is no question of the insured being obliged to pay an additional premium, if the trading results throw up a deficit. Moreover, the influence the body of the insured have over the management of these societies is negligible. Justification can therefore be found for making a distinction between these two kinds of insurance societies, by speaking of wholly mutual and semi-mutual societies. Our remarks refer exclusively to the former group.

One of the oldest forms of mutual insurance is that against fire. There is a strong sense of mutual solidarity in the case of *mutual fire insurance societies,* which, generally speaking, have only a limited field of operation. More than is the case with the large companies, their members are conscious of the fact that it is in their common interest to do their best to prevent fire damage. Since damage of this kind is often due to negligence or carelessness, and in the country often results, moreover, from fire breaking out in hay that has been stacked before it is properly dry — many farm fires in our pastureland areas are due to this — these local fire insurance societies exert a beneficial educational influence. A disadvantage of these small insurance societies is, however, that the risk has to be borne by a small number of members, which means that they have to re-insure themselves against risks to a greater extent than do larger companies.

The oldest mutual fire insurance societies date from the end of the 18th century; the majority of them, however, were founded during the second half of the 19th century and the first half of the 20th. In some areas these societies have retained their village character; in others their activities extend over a wider field and they have a large number of members. Their main activity is centred in the rural areas, where the majority of their members are farmers and market gardeners; only in a few towns are such societies of any significance.

Many mutual fire insurance societies do not confine insurance to damage from fire but have, in addition, one or more sections dealing with *storm damage, consequential losses and insurance covering glass, hail, war damage, burglary, hospital charges and cattle.* In general, however, mutual insurance against damage from hail is the concern of special societies, solely concerned with this type of assurance. Arable farmers and particularly market gardeners insure themselves for this purpose. Market gardeners are, of course, very much interested in insurance against damage to glass, part of the horticultural production of the Netherlands being carried on under glass. Cattle insurance is a characteristic form of insurance taken out by the small farmer, for whom the loss of an animal is a serious matter. Independent cattle funds are accordingly active chiefly in the areas of small farms. It is the custom of richer farmers owning animals of exceptionally high value (pedigree cattle, stud-horses) to insure these animals only.

Some of the mutual fire insurance societies have set up a mutual reinsurance society, while the others have taken out this form of insurance with private insurance companies.

In the Netherlands there are also various *mutual life assurance societies.* Two of these deserve special mention; they are particularly concerned with farming and both originated in the dairy farming sector. One was set up by co-operative dairy factories which desired to take out collective insurance on behalf of their personnel. The other resulted from the desire to take out life assurance policies on behalf of the members of co-operative dairy factories. In the meantime both organisations have widened their aim, making it possible for other co-operatives besides the dairy factories to insure their personnel or members, but their main activity still lies in the field of the dairy co-ops. It should also be mentioned that in the case of some dairy co-operatives the statutes even contain a clause to the effect that members automatically become insured by joining the co-operative. They are, however, always required to pay the necessary premium themselves and this payment is made by means of a deduction from the sum paid for milk delivered to the co-operative.

Mutual insurance comprises many *other forms,* all significant in themselves but not all of which can be discussed here. Suffice it to mention the existence of mutual insurance societies in the field of insurance against riot, transport insurance, insurance against liability for damage to third parties, insurance against employers' risks, ensuing from the various forms of compulsory social insurance, and the like. Some of these mutual insurance societies are of considerable size.

The *co-operative* idea has also found supporters *among the owners of small businesses,* whose bargaining position on the market is often weak for the same reasons as apply to the farmers. This is especially the case as regards the securing of credit by retail traders and craftsmen and the purchase of goods by small shopkeepers. The large banks were as little able to meet the credit requirements of these small traders and businessmen in a satisfactory fashion as they had been to meet the special requirements of agricultural credit. There is a strongly decentralised demand for credit in the case of small businesses too, and the question as to whether the borrower is reliable depends largely on personal qualities, which it is often difficult for an outsider to judge. The granting of credit to these people has, moreover, little attraction for the large commercial banks, since usually small sums only are involved.

The owners of small businesses have tried to meet their demand for credit — it is principally a demand for working, i.e. short-term, credit — by founding their own banks. Some of these banks were organised as co-operative societies, the liability of whose members was, in contrast to the farmers' credit banks, usually limited to a certain sum. These credit societies did not, however, meet with the same success as the farmers' creditbanks. This must be chiefly ascribed to the fact that the *middle class banks* [1]) were organised in three entirely separate groups. Once a single central bank had been set up in 1927, with financial help from the government, the organisation of this type of credit underwent an appreciable improvement and became of increasing importance. When this central bank was founded—it was called the Netherlands Middle Class Bank and was constituted as a limited company—most of the middle class banks already in existence were taken up into the new organisation as branch banks. Only a few of such banks remained on an independent footing, and most of these co-operate with the central bank. The independent banks include a number of co-operative banks.

The middle class banks are far less decentralised than are the farmers'

---

[1]) The term "middle class" here refers to the group of shopkeepers and owners of small private businesses.

credit banks. The Netherlands Middle Class Bank has about 80 branch banks. Even when one takes the independent banks into account the number of this type of local bank, when compared with the number of farmers' credit banks, cannot be termed other than small. But in considering this situation, it should be remembered that the owners of small businesses in the villages are often members of the farmers' credit banks and are provided with the necessary credit by these banks, while the owners of larger businesses can easily go to the large commercial banks for any credit they may need.

Since the beginning of this century shopkeepers have sought in increasing measure to collaborate in the form of *purchasing associations*. These associations are concerned with the joint purchase of articles traded by independent shopkeepers. This enables the joint body of shopkeepers to take large quantities of goods at one time from the wholesalers, thereby making it possible for them to secure rebates and other facilities regarding delivery and/or payment. The degree of collaboration varies considerably; sometimes the purchasing association has the legal character of a co-operative society, though in many cases it is a loose association without corporative status.

Purchasing associations are the most highly developed in the textile and grocery branches. They are, however, important in many other branches as well.

chapter VIII

Management and control

The *highest authority* within a co-operative society is the *general meeting of members*. This general meeting chooses the board of directors, which it can dismiss at any time. It can even amend the statutes, or rules, or decide to dissolve the co-operative, powers which no other organ within the co-operative society possesses.

In practice, however, it would be impossible to conduct business successfully, if the task of the general meeting were to be interpreted in such a manner that that body alone could take decisions, all the other organs merely playing an executive role. Consequently, it is the usual practice to place the *management* of a co-operative society in the hands of a *board of directors,* which board can in its turn appoint a manager responsible for part of the task of management.

This delegation of powers really amounts to a kind of *mandate*. On the one hand, the general meeting authorises the board of directors to take such steps as are desirable and necessary for the management of the co-operative, usually only important decisions — such as those relating to the purchase or sale of fixed assets, investments above a certain maximum, the raising of loans and the like — being reserved exclusively to the general meeting. Once every year, however, the board must report to the general meeting on the conduct of the society's affairs. On the other hand, the board charges the manager with the day-to-day administration, for which, however, the board itself remains responsible.

Here we strike up against a real difference between a co-operative society and a limited company. For, generally speaking, in the case of a limited company the administration is placed in the hands of one or more managers, supervised by a board of directors. This means that with a private company the managers, and not the board of directors, are responsible for the company's administration [1].

The principle whereby a co-operative society is managed by a board of

---

[1] We are aware that in the U.S.A. functions in a limited company are sometimes divided, the board of directors and in particular the president of the board carrying on the actual management, the managers occupying only a very subordinate position.

directors which employs one or more managers to assist it in the execution of its duties is applied almost everywhere in the world, though there are exceptions. Thus, in some cases, in the U.S.A. for example, the president or chairman of the co-operative is actually the managing director. His task is then a full-time job and he is remunerated accordingly. Another exception is met with in the Co-operative Wholesale Society in the U.K., which is managed by a board of 28 salaried directors to whom the managers of the various departments are responsible. In the Netherlands the law has associated itself with the practice generally adopted, by laying down explicitly in the Co-operative Societies Act that the board represents and manages the society. There is no mention even in this act of a manager as such.

A co-operative society can only operate satisfactorily if there is a *proper division of functions* between the board and the executive. Here we are concerned on the one hand with the relationship between the general meeting and the board and, on the other, with the division of functions between the board and the managers.

In the early days, when co-operative societies were small and relatively simple in their organisation, the general meeting did, in fact, exert a great deal of influence. This was only to be expected. It was not only that the guiding principle followed was that a co-operative is an association of individuals but—and this is more important—it was an easy thing in practice to convene all the members when an important decision had to be taken. Neither did the division of functions between the board and the manager give rise to much difficulty in the case of these small societies.

The division of functions between the various organs of a co-operative began to give rise to greater difficulty as the co-operatives increased in size, and as co-operatives began to be set up which were larger and more complicated from the very beginning. This produces two problems: the first relates to the function and significance of the general meeting, the other to the relationship between the board and the managers.

It is the duty of the board to present *a report and a statement of accounts to the general meeting of members,* relating to its conduct of the society's business. For this purpose, a general meeting must be held at least once a year. As a co-operative expands in size, however, the general meeting becomes less and less able to exercise the function for which it was originally designated. If all members attend the meeting, it takes on too massive a character for reasonable discussions to be held; but if most of the members stay away, the meeting is no longer truly representative. In either case the actual power of the board is much greater than was originally intended. Even its presentation of the report and statement of accounts threatens to become a mere announcement, accepted before the relevant documents have been properly studied.

63

If the general meeting is to function satisfactorily, a solution has to be found to this difficulty. The Netherlands Co-operative Societies Act accordingly provides for the setting up of a members' council. As will be explained in chapter XI, when discussing this act, there is an objection to this in that there is a danger of the members losing all direct contact with their board of directors. Consequently preference is often given to a regional grouping of members, the annual report and statement of accounts the board is to present to the general meeting and other matters then being informally discussed beforehand at regional meetings. It is true that in this way the general meeting tends to become a mere formality, but nevertheless, by means of these informal discussions prior to the holding of the general meeting the members do obtain a better insight into the scope of the decisions to be taken at that meeting.

It is the duty of the board of a co-operative society, not only at the general meeting but also during the course of the year, to assist members to form a reasonably good idea of the way the society's business is proceeding. This becomes all the more difficult the more complicated the commercial, financial and technical problems arising in the case of a large co-operative become. The members will only be able to form an opinion on such matters if the board provides them with *sufficient information.* This means that they must be regularly provided with news as to the society in good time and in ample measure. The *annual report,* in particular, must be of a high standard. It is also in the board's own interest that the general meeting should have some understanding of the way in which the business of the co-operative is being conducted, for the board is subordinate to the will of the body of members, and especially when trading results are not too favourable, it is important for it to know that it enjoys the members' confidence.

Nevertheless, even when the board does supply the general meeting with liberal information, in many cases a need is still felt for a *supervisory council,* expressly for the purpose of subjecting the annual report and statement of accounts to proper study. In the case of small co-operatives, where even a layman is able to understand the administration, the general meeting can obtain sufficient information about the board's report and statement of accounts from a finance committee, set up especially for the purpose of controlling the accounting. On the basis of its findings, the finance committee advises the general meeting whether or not to accept the annual report and statement of accounts, or whether to bring up certain matters for discussion. A finance committee of this nature, being appointed anew and composed of different members every year, cannot, however, obtain a proper insight into the board's management of affairs, once the co-operative has grown to any size. In this case a permanent supervisory council, which is kept regularly informed of the society's position by the board, is a far better proposition. Consequently, in our country the finance committees have gradually made way for supervisory councils, at least in the larger co-operative societies.

The task of the supervisory council is by no means an easy one. It should confine itself to the main lines of management but often it wants a full exchange of ideas with the board regarding even minor decisions taken by this latter body and calls for meetings with the board for this purpose. On the other hand, it sometimes happens that the supervisory council places too much confidence in the board and fails to form an objective opinion of its conduct of business even on important points.

Although a supervisory council may be better informed, like the finance committee, in forming its opinion it has nevertheless to depend on the assistance of *an accountant*. At present the administration of most co-operative societies in the Netherlands is audited and examined by the accounting section of their central organisations. This inspection is not confined to the accounting but very often covers organisational matters as well. A number of co-operative societies in the Netherlands, however, make use of the services of a private accountant's office.

The central organisations, of course, make use of private accountants for this purpose, and it is customary for the larger co-operatives to do likewise. Since the co-operative movement in our country is characterised by the consistent application of the voluntary principle, every co-operative society is free to have its auditing done by whatever body it, wisely or unwisely, prefers, though the statutes of some of the central organisations prescribe that membership involves a liability to submit to audit by, or on behalf of, the central organisation. It should be mentioned that, generally speaking, audit by private firms of accountants is of a very high standard in the Netherlands.

The following may be said of the second problem that arises when the co-operative takes on larger proportions, i.e. that concerning the division of functions between the board and *the manager*. In the case of small co-operative societies the board is fully conversant with the running of the society, down to the smaller details. In fact, the board forms the management and the manager is really the bookkeeper, who, as managing clerk, is also charged with the daily conduct of business. The task of the boards of the large industrial and commercial co-operatives, which developed at a later date, is naturally far more difficult than that of the boards of small local co-operatives, and the need to leave part of the day-to-day administration in the hands of a manager much greater. Thus a co-operative dairy factory can only function satisfactorily if the day-to-day management is in the hands of a man who knows how milk has to be processed to produce dairy products of good quality and how to attract first-class skilled labour, who is trained in administration, and who—if the local dairy does not happen to be associated with a marketing co-operative—knows how to sell his products. And an egg-marketing co-operative will not be able to compete on the market, if selling is entrusted to a manager who proves to be no salesman. But a board of a dairy co-operative, consisting of farmers, is in no position to give instructions to the manager on the production process and on the most efficient organisation of the work; while the board of an egg-marketing co-operative is obliged to leave egg sales to a manager.

All this means that the function of the manager in a co-operative society is becoming constantly more important. In many cases this has given rise to a difficult situation, since whereas the board is still regarded as the managing body, in reality it is not in a position to exercise the function of management, at least, not with regard to important sections of the work. In some cases, in fact, the manager and not the board conducts the co-operative, the board being relegated to a position similar to that of a board of directors in a limited company. In such cases, the position has, indeed, become the same, in practice and juridically, as that in a limited company. In other cases, however, the manager is hampered in the performance of his duties by the board's tendency to concern itself with too many details. As a result, decisions are held up, and this has an unfavourable influence on the co-operative's competitive position on the market. There is a danger, moreover, of the manager losing much of the pleasure he takes in his work.

There are *three conditions for a satisfactory division of functions* between the board and the manager. The first is that they should work together in an atmosphere of *mutual confidence*. If such confidence is lacking, or insufficient, the co-operative is doomed to inevitable failure. Of course much will depend on the board finding a suitable person to fill the role of manager, for which job the essential requirements are professional skill and character. Important considerations should be how far this official is prepared to regard himself as the co-operative's servant and whether he is aware that he must manage affairs according to the views of the board. If he is unable to, then he is not fitted to fill a managerial function in the co-operative.

Another condition is that *the board* should be kept *fully informed* by the manager of all decisions taken. This implies that the manager should systematically supply his board with information regarding his execution of the task entrusted to him, in doing which he should endeavour to achieve as great an objectivity as possible; for as soon as the board were to form the impression that any mistakes he might have made were being concealed from them, this would undermine their confidence in him and hamper collaboration between them. The manager should remember that only weak officials feel a need to give a one-sided account of their work. Devotion and perfect open-heartedness, combined with efficiency, form the basis for the satisfactory fulfilment of the task a manager of a co-operative society has to perform.

And a third condition is that a division of functions between the board and the manager should be sought, whereby *organisational policy* remains *in the hands of the board,* while the manager is left a wide measure of freedom as regards commercial policy, staffing matters and the actual production process. Nevertheless, in these matters too, the board should as far as possible indicate the main lines of policy. As for financial policy, this should be decided upon by mutual consultation between board and manager.

Good management requires that *the board should be a small one.* For it has to meet frequently—regular meetings are an important factor —and it needs to be able to arrive at decisions quickly. If, for one reason or another, a large board is desired, it is advisable for it to appoint an executive committee, consisting preferably of three of its members.

It is, of course, obvious that the division of functions between the board and the manager of a co-operative society is determined in the main by the personal qualities of the persons concerned. There can be no question of a board truly exercising the function of management, if its members are unequipped for the task.

Since, generally speaking, there is a danger that the influence a board exerts over the management of a co-operative is insufficient, great attention is paid in countries where the co-operative movement is highly developed to the *training of board members.* Here we would point to Sweden in particular, where there is an excellent training college for prospective board members for the agricultural co-operatives. Similar institutes exist in other countries as well. At the same time, in many countries one meets with organised courses, more or less decentralised in character. This is the case in the Netherlands.

Good board directors are few and far between and this applies parti-cularly to the presidents or chairmen. For this reason it has gradually become the practice in several countries to grant board members some *compensation* for the work they do. The central organisations and some of the large co-operatives in the Netherlands sometimes grant board members some modest remuneration; the chairman's remuneration will often be more or less in keeping with the time he devotes to the co-operative's work. The members of the boards—and also the chairmen —of the thousands of local co-operatives in our country are practically all unpaid.

It has already been said that the members of the board are chosen by the general meeting of members. A general meeting, however, is not always in a position to make a sufficiently sharp distinction between men, who, by a certain eloquence, try to create the impression that they would be eminently suitable for duties on the board, and those who are so suited, though they have less to say for themselves. Under these circumstances, it is perfectly understandable that in nominating candidates at the general meeting, a certain influence should be brought to bear by the board recommending the meeting to vote for a given candidate. However, it should never be forgotten that one can easily go too far in this respect.

chapter IX

Organisation

It seems useful to devote a separate chapter to a number of problems that concern the way the co-operative movement in our country is organised. Some aspects of its organisation have already been discussed in the foregoing chapters. We have devoted a separate chapter (chapter VIII) to the internal organisation of a co-operative society, where the main problem is that of the division of functions among the various organs of the society. In this chapter we shall be more particularly interested in the problem of the specialised and the multi-purpose co-operative, the question whether dealings with non-members are admissible, the extent to which members should be free, under all circumstances, to join and to leave the society, and whether they should be compelled to make use of the services the co-operative has to offer. We shall also devote attention in this chapter to the relationship between the local co-operatives and their central organisations and will also attempt to give the reader an impression of the over-all picture presented by the joint organisations of groups of co-operatives in our country, though in view of the limited space at our command, we shall naturally be unable to go into this matter fully.

First of all, then, the question wether *the specialised or the multi-purpose co-operative* is to be preferred. It will be clear from the foregoing chapters that in our country the specialised co-operative is the rule and the multi-purpose co-operative the exception, the main reason for this being that the co-operative societies were set up by certain groups—farmers, market gardeners, consumers, shopkeepers—with the aim of bettering their position in society. These co-operatives were local in character; they were founded as a result of local enterprise and bore the marked character of associations of persons who all knew each other. Their aims were different, of course, and the types of business they ran also displayed wide variety. The establishment of the first horticultural auction society in 1887, for instance, came about entirely independently of the founding of the first co-operative dairy factory in 1886, and this first co-operative dairy factory was established without being connected in any way with the founding of the first agricultural supply co-op in 1877. The establishment of the first consumers' co-operative bore no relation to what was taking place in the field of the agricultural co-operatives, for these two types of co-operative had differing aims and leadership was in the hands of entirely different groups of interests.

Naturally, when setting up new co-operatives account was taken of the experience already gained and this was obviously all the more so, the more similarity there was in the aims of the local co-operatives. This provides the explanation of the growing degree of co-operation between local co-operatives in the various sectors (consumers' co-operatives, co-operative dairy factories, supply co-ops, co-operative banks). It was therefore not long before groups of similar co-operatives were forming central organisations, which "top" co-operatives were consequently specialised organisations as well.

This specialisation becomes all the more understandable if three factors are taken into consideration.

In the first place, the optimum operational area of the one type of co-operative can be appreciably smaller than that of another type. A farmers' credit bank must be fairly small in size; a co-operative sugar factory operates over a much wider field. The second reason is that different groups of farmers cultivate different products and employ different machines and other farming requisites. The producers of seed potatoes usually have few poultry; the majority of poultry farmers do not also cultivate seed potatoes. And the final factor is that some activities cannot easily be combined in one co-operative. Thus, generally speaking, it is not advisable to include different types of processing within one co-operative.

On the other hand, there are some factors which make for a combination of functions. Often, for example, the interests of members do run parallel, which may lead to the establishment of co-operatives which concern themselves both with the purchase of farming requisites and with the sale of certain farming products. This combination may have resulted from the initiative and influence of one of the leading members of the co-operative; or it may have developed gradually, the original aim having been limited and the co-operative extending its activity, according to need, as time went on.

It cannot be denied that the combining of various aims in one society has its advantages. Such advantages are all the more important if the business of the specialised co-operative were on so small a scale that it would be difficult to find a capable manager and no satisfactory division of labour in the business and office would be possible. Moreover, it is not easy to find suitable board members for all these small co-operatives. If there is a smaller number of co-operatives on a broader scale, it is, of course, sufficient to have fewer board members. And, finally, favourable trading results achieved in one department of a multi-purpose co-

70

operative can be employed to support a new enterprise, which otherwise could not be undertaken.

One disadvantage that can arise in the case of the multi-purpose co-operative is that the accounts of the different departments are not kept sufficiently separate, so that one cannot know precisely how each department is doing. Also, the day-to-day management threatens to become too decentralised, if departments exist side by side which actually bear little relation to each other.

Although there are only a few multi-purpose co-operatives in the Netherlands, there are some that have been most successful. As far as the combination of aims is concerned, in our country you can find co-operatives which perform both the function of farmers' credit bank and of supply co-op, and a co-operative dairy factory may also take charge of the purchase of farming requisites for its members. The combination of an agricultural purchasing co-operative with a consumers' co-operative is rare. It is much more usual for an agricultural purchasing co-operative to concern itself with the sale of various agricultural products on behalf of its members.

Just one or two remarks on the question of *dealings with non-members*. As a co-operative society is an association of individuals, this implies that, in principle, its activities are restricted to its members. Nevertheless, there are circumstances in which dealings with non-members can be justified. This is why in the Netherlands Co-operative Societies Act it is stated explicitly that a co-operative does not lose its essential character, if its statutes contain a clause whereby its activities can be extended to third parties.

The reason why a co-operative sometimes does business with non-members is that in this way its competitive power is supposed to be strengthened. One should imagine a co-operative dairy factory with too small a turnover to be able to compete well on the market. Propaganda will be carried on to persuade farmers supplying milk to join the co-operative, but this propaganda may be unsuccessful. Rational and irrational objections have to be overcome. One way is to allow prospective members to have their milk processed by the co-operative, by way of trial; perhaps when the trial period comes to an end, they will decide to join. Moreover—and this is more significant—in this way the co-operative obtains a larger turnover, which increases its ability to compete on the market. Although it is understandable that co-operatives should adopt this method of obtaining new members, there is a disadvantage attached to this form of propaganda. Few farmers supplying milk will want to become members of the co-operative under these circumstances, as they obtain the same price for their milk as that received by the members, without having to accept the financial responsibility for any eventual deficit. The consequence may be that new members fail to join, the old members die out; as the number of members declines, the liability per member increases and the co-operative becomes "hollowed out", as it were. Those in our country, who proceed from the principle that a co-operative should limit its activities to its members and who are aware of the danger that threatens when dealings with non-members begin to assume considerable proportions, have taken a stand against this phenomenon, which in some sectors has assumed larger proportions than is thought desirable.

A solution to this difficulty must be sought on the one hand in systematic propaganda, aimed at inducing non-members to accept membership and at making the board-members of the co-operatives concerned fully conscious of the dangers inherent to large-scale dealings with non-members. On the other hand, a more satisfactory situation could be got by discriminating between members and non-members as regards the prices paid for produce received and the prices charged for requisites delivered. In those cases in which the co-operative's competitive position is weak, it is naturally difficult for it to apply a policy of price discrimination, since this might alienate non-members, on whose deliveries and/or purchases the co-operative depends.

As has already been said often before, the co-operative movement in the Netherlands is, generally speaking, characterised by the application of the principle of freedom and by the absence of compulsion. A characteristic feature in this respect is *freedom to join or to leave the co-operative*. Such freedom is explicitly and emphatically laid down in the Netherlands Co-operative Societies Act, though this does not preclude the introduction of conditions governing entry and withdrawal.

The application of the principle of open membership in the case of co-operation is not in itself by any means obvious. If a group of people decide to do business on a co-operative basis, it would be quite understandable, if, as soon as the business proved successful, they should decide to bar the entry of new members or to make further membership subject to certain restrictive conditions. The co-operative movement, however, has, in general, accepted the free accession of new members, the principle of open membership having even been regarded as an essential feature of the movement. One can even say that, as the admission of new members is deliberately excluded, the enterprise loses its co-operative character, and all that remains is an undertaking, the characteristic feature of which is that it is run by a restricted number of suppliers of the raw material or buyers of the finished products.

To an extent the application of open membership can be regarded as an indication of the idealistic character of the co-operative movement. Moreover, in many cases the entry of new members has strengthened

72

Consumers' co-operatives have their own factories

Dutch farmers have built a co-operative factory for the production of fertilizers

A co-operative shop

A new co-operative activity in the Netherlands: locker plants

the co-operative and was therefore looked upon as being in its own interest. It might also be remarked that often few or no disadvantages are attached to open membership. Nevertheless circumstances may arise in which it is judged essential to admit new members only on certain conditions and there is no doubt at all that, provided that the nature of the co-operative concerned demands it, the attaching of conditions to admission is acceptable.

In general, the principle of open membership is accepted in the Netherlands, though in most cases a small entry fee is required. For the rest, in most cases the statutes of co-operative societies contain a clause to the effect that membership is dependent upon one's sharing the common interest of the society. Thus co-operative dairy factories always restrict membership to farmers keeping dairy cattle, and in the statutes of all co-operative auction societies one finds a clause to the effect that only market gardeners can become members.

While in the foregoing cases, there is hardly any question of a condition attached to admission into a co-operative society, the situation is rather different in the case of some processing co-operatives. We have already pointed out that processing co-operatives which work with shares, to which a liability to deliver produce is attached, can indeed accept new shareholders, but that these new members often have to pay more than the nominal price for their shares. The attachment of conditions to the entry of new members in this sense is not regarded in the Netherlands as being in conflict with the essential character of the co-operative, as formulated in the Co-operative Societies Act.

As regards freedom to withdraw from membership of a co-operative society, the Co-operative Societies Act expressly states that this freedom is not nullified, if conditions are attached to it which are in accord with the aim and purport of the society concerned. Unrestricted freedom to withdraw can, of course, have serious consequences for a co-operative in which much capital is invested. For in these cases, if members were to withdraw for some reason or other, the turnover would decline and this decline in turnover would necessarily result in less satisfactory returns, since the overhead costs are high. Generally speaking, therefore, co-operatives operating with low overhead costs are more inclined to apply the principle of free withdrawal, without any conditions attached, than are those operating with high overhead costs.

It is not possible to give a general answer to the question as to how far conditions attached to withdrawal must be regarded as in accord with the aim and purport of the society concerned or not. A guarantee against abuse in this respect is that according to the Dutch law, the memorandum of association of new co-operatives has to be submitted to a notary, whose job it is to form an opinion as to the admissibility of the desired provisions in the statutes regarding conditions of withdrawal. This also applies to changes in the statutes of existing societies. The notary will naturally take full account of the nature of the co-operative and particularly of the amount of capital investment involved in coming to his opinion as to whether the conditions of withdrawal are acceptable.

There is a close connection between the problem of freedom to withdraw and the *obligation to make use of the co-operative.*

The effect of the obligation to make use of the co-operative is, indeed, largely determined by the conditions for withdrawal. If a member of a co-operative is obliged to make use of the co-operative's services but can withdraw from membership at any time he may wish, such withdrawal would also put an end to his obligation. If, on the other hand, the conditions attached to withdrawal are such that they make it extremely difficult for a member to withdraw, the clause obliging him to make use of the co-operative's services retains its force. If, however, the co-operative is of the kind which does not oblige its members to make use of its services, it does not matter to the member whether onerous conditions are attached to withdrawal or not. One can always remain a member without doing any business with the co-operative.

In general, what was said above regarding the possibility of withdrawing from a co-operative applies also to the obligation to make use of its services: co-operatives employing a large amount of capital and therefore having high overhead costs will be more inclined to include the obligation to use the co-operative in their statutes than co-operatives employing only a small amount of capital. We have already mentioned in chapter V that in the case of many processing co-operatives the obligation to make use of a co-operative is coupled to the possession of one or more shares. Withdrawal from these co-operatives is only permitted if one can manage to get others, whom the co-operative will accept as new members, to take over one's shares.

Moreover, the application of the members' obligation to deliver the goods they produce to the co-operative or to take their farming requisites from the co-operative has to be made dependent on the possibility of a check to see that such a provision is observed and the possibility of applying sanctions in case of inobservance. If it is difficult to detect inobservance of such a provision, then it is better that it should not be applied at all; but if control is possible, then an obligation of this kind could be included in the statutes. Much depends, too, on the value attributed to such obligations and on their psychological effect. If provisions of this nature were to have an unfavourable psychological effect on the members, then it is advisable, for that reason, not to make the use of the co-operative compulsory, but to try to achieve the same result by means of propaganda. The members' trade with the co-operative can, moreover, be stimulated by making their share in any financial surplus

74

to be apportioned among them dependent upon the extent to wich they have traded with the co-operative. As has already been mentioned in chapter VI, such a provision is met with in the case of the central organisation of the consumers' co-operatives. In determining the degree of "loyalty" to the co-operative, the actual amount taken from the central organisation is, of course, compared against the amount that could have been taken, if the central society's whole range of products had been made use of.

In the case of some forms of co-operatives there is definitely a good case for including in the statutes an obligation to make use of the co-operative. This is particularly so with marketing co-operatives, for here there is a danger that members might otherwise only make use of the co-operative's services when persuaded to by the state of the market. For, if the market is brisk, the individual seller has little difficulty in marketing his produce, and members of a co-operative then often show a tendency to sell to private dealers. If, however, the market is slack and private dealers are not buying much, members prefer to put their produce at the disposal of the co-operative. When trade is slack, it is difficult for a marketing co-operative, however, to find a market for a supply in excess of what its regular customers are in the habit of taking. Members of co-operatives also often show a tendency to sell special products in great demand to private dealers and to send those for which there is less demand to the co-operative. This is no use to the co-operative either. Consequently, marketing co-operatives, even when their overhead costs are not high, have often included explicit provisions in their statutes obliging the members to make use of the co-operative.

In the Netherlands the use made of conditions attached to withdrawal from a co-operative shows great diversity, as does also the application of the rule making it obligatory for members to make use of their co-operative. Here is not the place, however, for a detailed survey of the ways in which these principles are applied in the various sectors of the co-operative movement.

Next, a few remarks about *the relation between local or regional co-operatives and the central organisations* of which they form part, (the term "local" or "regional" being used according to the area they cover). In dealing with this matter, we shall be able at the same time to give a general sketch of the organisation of the co-operative movement in the Netherlands.

The organisation of the co-operatives in the Netherlands shows little over-all plan or uniformity and accordingly does not present a very clear picture. This is to be attributed to the spontaneous development of the movement in our country. We have already pointed out that a large number of central organisations of groups of similar co-operative societies gradually came into being, all of which have different aims and are different in character.

Some of these central organisations are non-commercial societies, that is "unions", whose purpose it is to furnish their members with advice on legal, organisational, fiscal and technical matters; the others do business and are concerned with wholesaling, processing or manufacturing. Sometimes one finds one or more non-commercial unions and one or more central commercial organisations in the same sector. In other sectors, however, both types of organisation are joined together, so that the central organisation is not only doing business, but also renders those services to its members which are normally the concern of a union. In the dairy sector, for instance, we find regional unions of co-operative dairy factories, joined together in a national organisation of federal character. Side by side with these, however, co-operatives have been set up for the marketing of the products of local dairy co-operatives affiliated to them, and these central marketing co-operatives have, in their turn, set up a non-commercial union. An example of the combination of both functions —that of a union and of a business organisation—is provided by the Central Society of Netherlands Consumers' Co-operatives, which devotes itself on the one hand to the wholesale trade and even to production on behalf of local consumers' co operatives, and on the other hand affords these local co-operatives the necessary technical, organisational, legal and fiscal assistance. This organisation is, moreover, highly centralised, since there are no regional organisations operating between itself and the local co-operatives.

Another important point is the extent to which the "primary" co-operatives prove ready to grant the central organisation to which they belong a large measure of influence. If a central organisation consists of many small local societies, circumstances can more easily lead to a transfer of certain powers to the central organisation than in the case of a national organisation consisting of a few very large co-operatives. This is one of the reasons why in our country the influence exercised by the two central banks over the local farmers' credit banks is far greater than the influence the Union of Co-operative Sugar Factories has over its members. This difference cannot be attributed exclusively to the fact that there are about 1,300 farmers' credit banks and only 6 co-operative sugar factories in our country, for the significance of the central organisation depends first and foremost upon the importance of the central organisation to the member co-operative, and this in its turn is determined by the function the central organisation fulfils. We may take as an example the technical advice that certain non-commercial organisations give their members, advice which is sometimes practically indispensable to the local co-operative concerned. Another example is the administrative and organisational control that central organisations exercise over local co-operatives and which the members of these local co-operatives look upon as a guarantee of good management. However, not all the various central organisations perform the same functions and these differences partly explain the varying degree of influence the central organisations have over their members.

Furthermore, the way the central organisations develop is often determined by the personal influence of their leaders. In fact, the success of the co-operative often depends on a few exponents in leading positions. At the same time the organisation of the co-operative movement in our country is strongly influenced by the fact that separate co-operatives have been founded by various groups of people sharing the same philosophy of life, membership actually being confined to these categories. This influence has played its rôle in the case of the organisation of credit co-operatives for instance. We have two central co-operative farmers' credit banks in our country, the one being the representative of a large number of local farmers' credit banks formed almost exclusively by Roman Catholic farmers and market gardeners, the other being of more general character. It is, however, remarkable that this phenomenon is not found in every sector. It is characteristic of the organisation of agricultural purchasing co-operatives but not of the co-operative dairy industry, characteristic of the organisation of the cattle-marketing and meat-processing co-operatives but not of the consumers' co-operatives. It would take us too far, however, to go into the reasons for this.

A word about the relationship between agricultural co-operatives and farmers' unions.

In the Netherlands the farmers are organized in three farmers' unions, based on different convictions. These are a Roman Catholic, a Protestant and a general farmers' union.

Although the majority of the members of the Protestant and general farmers' union are in sympathy with the co-operative idea and although they have repeatedly taken the initiative to set up co-operatives—the general farmers' union especially—there is no organizational link between them and the agricultural co-operatives. Accordingly, the co-operatives in the areas where the two farmers' unions are active exist quite separately from them. This does not, of course, prevent exponents of both farmers' organizations from often playing an important rôle as members of the boards of agricultural co-operatives.

The relationship between the Roman Catholic farmers' union and the co-operatives is entirely different. Particularly in those areas where the population is almost exclusively Catholic, a close bond exists between various co-operatives and the Roman Catholic union, which has very often provided the stimulus for their foundation. On the one hand most of these agricultural co-operatives restrict their membership to members of the farmers' union, while the latter, on the other hand, are often allowed to exert a certain influence on the co-operatives' policy.

This form of co-operation undoubtedly has certain advantages. In the first place the management of the co-operatives and that of the farmers' unions share one and the same outlook, which strengthens the position of both. In the second place, the co-operatives have very often assumed responsibility for assisting the farmers' union financially, so that the latter has more funds at its disposal for undertaking various activities on its members' behalf.

Mention should also be made of the *institutes for agricultural co-operatives*.

Since a growing need was felt in various parts of our country for more intensive collaboration between co-operatives in the field of propaganda and information, groups of agricultural co-operatives of various nature have set up regional institutes for agricultural co-operatives. The work of these institutes has not remained confined to propaganda and information, for as time has gone on more and more attention has been paid to the training of prospective board members for the local co-operatives.

Finally, a few remarks about the *National Co-operative Council* (Nationale Coöperatieve Raad). Until the year 1934 there was no organisation in the Netherlands that could be regarded as the sole representative of the entire co-operative movement in our country. There was apparently no real need for such an organisation at the time. This is understandable if one takes into account the fact that the various central organisations often pursued entirely different aims, only contacting each other, if there was some special reason for doing so. Another important factor was that in the past the government pursued a passive economic policy. It was not until a change came about in this situation during the 'thirties that the co-operatives had more common interests to defend. Gradually the need for regular contact increased and this led in 1934 to the setting up—by the central organisations of the agricultural purchasing co-operatives, the consumers' co-operatives and the farmers' credit banks—of the National Co-operative Council. The number of member organisations belonging to the Council gradually increased in the ensuing years. Nowadays all central organisations of co-operatives are affiliated to the Council, one of the tasks of which organisation is to promote the joint interests of co-operative societies in the Netherlands. Its most important function, however, is to represent the co-operative movement and to carry on propaganda.

chapter X

Financing the co-operatives

Co-operation, in the sense in which we are using it here, means conducting business on a co-operative basis. The question of the financing of the co-operative society ought, therefore, to be seen in the light of the problem of financing businesses in general.

Briefly, the principles that have to be borne in mind in financing business amount to the following. A distinction should be made between the need for long-term capital and the need for short-term capital. Long-term capital serves to finance the fixed assets—such as land, buildings and machines—a certain minimum quantity of raw materials, auxiliary materials and finished products, permanent cash requirements and regularly outstanding claims.

Long-term capital requirements can be met both by a firm's own capital and by attracting capital from outside. But it is always a condition that the amount borrowed should be at the borrower's disposal for a lengthy period. This can be arranged in various ways, e.g. by a money loan raised on mortgage, by the issue of debentures and so on.

Short-term capital requirements depend mainly on fluctuations in the total working capital during the course of the production process. Some businesses need the same amount of working capital all the year through, while in others the need for such capital shows marked seasonal variation.

Fluctuations in capital requirements above a certain minimum can best be financed by means of short-term loans. The use of short-term credit is all the more justified, the more temporary the need for it is. The form of credit most adaptable to fluctuations in the demand for it is the bank loan, especially a loan on current account.

It is difficult to say what ratio should be maintained between a firm's own capital and outside capital, since it is necessary to take a number of requirements into account, especially as regards profitability and solvency.

The businessman, for whom financing is partly a question of costs, will naturally ask himself what ratio between his own capital and capital from outside is most profitable. If his firm's chances of making a profit are favourable and the interest charged on outside capital relatively low, his own capital will yield the greatest return if it represents only a small part of the total working capital. If the chances of making a profit are small, however, a large amount of borrowed capital represents considerable fixed costs, which has an unfavourable effect on the returns from the firm's own capital. Generally speaking, therefore, the businessman inclined to speculation, who is on the look out for maximum profits and who does not attach a great deal of importance to the risk of incurring a loss, will prefer to do business using only a small amount of own capital. The more sober-minded businessman, who is wide-awake to the risk of losses, will, on the other hand, regard capital from outside as a necessary evil.

Every businessman who attaches great importance to solvency will regard it as essential, from the point of view of sound financing, that his own capital should represent a reasonable portion of his total working capital. Here the principle on which one generally works is that the firm's own capital should cover the largest possible amount of its constant capital requirements. If a firm starts out with a comparatively small amount of its own capital and a large amount of borrowed capital, the ratio can gradually be improved to the advantage of the former by building up the firm's own capital holding. To achieve this a conservative write-off policy should be adopted, and any profit should, as far as possible, be ploughed back into the business. As its own capital increases, the firm can redeem its capital loans from outside. Here we have left out of account any demand for capital due to the expansion of the firm.

The same problems arise as regards financing in a co-operative as in every other enterprise. A co-operative's working capital needs not consist entirely of its own holdings either, and it is also true in the case of the co-operative that the greater the fluctuations in its capital requirements, the more desirable it is to borrow capital from outside.

But it is important to state at the outset that it is not the aim of a co-operative society to obtain the greatest possible return on the capital invested in it. On the contrary, its aim is to do business on its members' behalf, or, if one prefers, to promote its members' interests, the financing simply being a necessary consequence of such activity. This is why a co-operative society does not, in principle, endeavour to raise profits to as high a level as possible by employing as much outside capital as it can. This method of financing a co-operative is altogether undesirable, in fact, since the aim should be to put the undertaking on as stable a footing as possible. Accordingly, a co-operative society should preferably endeavour to employ a relatively large proportion of its own capital as working capital.

Now, it is a well-known fact that co-operatives are often set up by groups of people who have little capital at their disposal. This has given rise to a problem as regards financing, for, while a co-operative should dispose of a relatively large amount of own capital, the circumstances were such that this capital could not be furnished by its members. For these members either did not possess any capital or, if they did, often could not release it from the service it was performing on their own farms in order to finance the proposed co-operative.

The way this problem was solved in our country can, perhaps, best be shown by giving a concrete example, that provided by the first co-operative dairy factory in the Netherlands. The circumstances in which this co-operative was set up, were described in chapter V.

The cattle farmers who decided upon the founding of this *first co-operative dairy factory* were all tenant-farmers and had insufficient funds to set up a dairy factory. Their money was invested in their farms and was often not sufficient for financing these either. The problem of financing this first co-operative dairy factory was solved by framing statutes which included two provisions, making it possible to issue a debenture loan.

The first provision was concerned with the members' liability towards the co-operative. The founders of this first co-operative dairy factory accepted the principle that no one could become a member of the co-operative unless he was prepared to accept unlimited liability for its commitments. The second provision obliged the members to deliver all the milk they had available to the co-operative factory. The significance of this second provision is clear, for there would have been no point in building a co-operative dairy factory as long as there was a possibility of the members processing the milk on their own farms — and they had, of course, the necessary skill and equipment to do this — whenever they saw an opportunity to do so. If they were to have done this, it would have meant that every now and again the co-operative dairy factory would either have had to remain idle or obtain milk from other sources.

It is clear that the members' acceptance of the principle of unlimited liability and the obligation to deliver milk made it simpler to obtain the loan required to build the factory. For although the members were not able to put their money down on the table to finance their co-operative, they did possess capital, though this was locked up in their farms. Thus the total liability of the members as a body provided the lenders of the capital with a guarantee that they would get their money back, even should the new undertaking prove a failure.

In addition, the provision regarding the compulsory use of the co-operative made it an easy matter to pay the interest on, and to redeem the debenture loan, the sums required for this purpose being regarded as working costs. It is true that this forced down the price the co-operative paid for milk delivered to it, but this did not mean that its members turned elsewhere, since they had already accepted the obligation to deliver their milk to the co-operative factory, whatever the financial consequences. Naturally this meant that the members could not be allowed to withdraw from membership of the co-operative as they liked, and withdrawal was accordingly made subject to certain conditions in the society's statutes.

But in the final analysis interest in the co-operative depends on the price paid for the milk delivered, and if this price had remained unsatisfactory, the first co-operative dairy factory would not have been a success. That it was a success is evidenced by the great development this branch of co-operative activity has undergone.

It may be mentioned that the debenture loan issued by the first co-operative dairy factory in the Netherlands was taken up chiefly by the more well-to-do inhabitants of the village and its environments, who were anxious to support the experiment. Landowners, the majority of whom happened to reside in another part of the country, also helped to make this co-operative a success and to bring about a highly necessary improvement in the farmers' economic position by purchasing the debenture bonds.

So much for the financing of the first co-operative dairy factory. Now a word about the financing of this kind of co-operative, once the first phase of development was over.

By applying the financial policy described earlier on, the co-operative was able gradually to redeem the debenture loan. The conditions for raising a new debenture loan were then more favourable than at the start, for the co-operative had in the meantime proved its viability. When it was necessary to renew and expand equipment, it was an easy matter to attract a new loan on the same basis.

Besides paying off the debenture loan, the co-operative formed its own capital holding by applying a deliberate write-off policy and by building up reserves. Nevertheless, the financing of the co-operative dairy industry by means of debenture loans or bank loans has retained its significance up to the present day.

It would be incorrect, however, to think that the method employed to finance the first co-operative dairy factory was also applied in founding other processing co-operatives. In order to make it clear why a different course was followed in the case of other processing co-operatives, we shall now describe how the *first co-operative beet sugar factory* was set up in our country in 1899.

Without going here into the motives which led to the setting up of the co-operative sugar factories (see chapter V), it can be said that in founding such factories one was confronted with problems different in nature from those that had arisen when founding the first co-operative dairy factory. In the first place a sugar factory is much larger than a dairy factory. Since milk soon spoils and can only be transported over comparatively short distances without causing a considerable diminution in quality, the dairy industry is highly decentralised, consisting of small units which require comparatively little capital investment. A beet sugar factory, on the other hand, requires a large concentration of capital and must itself be of large size, if it is going to pay. Its operational area is accordingly wider and the bond uniting its members, who live far apart from one another, weaker than that uniting the members of a local co-operative dairy factory. Since the members do not know each other so well, they are less able to judge one another's solvency. But, in the second place, the founding of the first co-operative sugar factory was much more of an experiment for, in contrast to dairying, a process was involved with which the farmers were unfamiliar.

It was due to these two circumstances that the enterprise was not financed on the basis of unlimited liability. Accordingly, for sugar-processing a co-operative society was arrived at on the basis of shares combined with limited liability. As a rule, these shares had a nominal value of 500 guilders, of which amount about 100 guilders was paid up. Liability, moreover, was often not limited to the amount of the shares, but exceeded it. Although efforts were made to sell a large number of shares before it was definitely decided to set up the factory, the total capital subscribed finally proved to be only a mere fraction of the total amount of working capital required, the sum being even insufficient to finance the construction of a factory and the purchase of machinery.

Naturally this was no basis for attracting the loans required to finance the enterprise as a whole. A factory is, of course, a suitable object for raising a money loan on mortgage, but a sugar mill that has no earning power has no liquidation value worth speaking of. Consequently the amount of credit that could be procured on such security was inadequate to cover the rest of the capital requirements. The founders of the first co-operative sugar factory also endeavoured, therefore, to increase the solvency of the new enterprise by making it compulsory for the members to make use of the co-operative. There was the more reason for doing this, since a sugar factory requires large capital investment, so that if the turnover falls to any considerable extent below working capacity, great losses are incurred.

Now, a clause in the statutes obliging the members to put all their beets at the factory's disposal could not be regarded as an adequate solution. Much more effective is a clause whereby the possession of a share involves a liability to deliver a certain minimum quantity of the raw material to the co-operative every year, for in this way a member is forced to cultivate beets, whatever the circumstances, if he does not want to be obliged to buy them.

Since the yield of beets per acre varies from year to year, it was decided to oblige the shareholder to deliver a minimum quantity per annum; but a maximum limit to the amount he could deliver to the factory was also laid down. The number of shares members took was determined, inter alia, by the number of acres they wanted to devote to the cultivation of beets.

By including in the statutes a clause whereby members could only withdraw from the co-operative society by transferring, with the approval of the board, their share to others, it was ensured that the secession of members dit not lead to a proportionate decline in the supply of the raw material, for the new owner of the share took over from the previous owner the obligations attached to it. It may be remarked in passing that these obligations had an influence on the price paid for shares so transferred. A share which entails the obligation to deliver beets to a co-operative which is not operating on a competitive basis is naturally less attractive than one that entitles one to deliver beets to a co-operative paying a highly competitive price for them.

This scheme, i.e. share capital and the compulsory delivery of a quantity of the raw material by members, proportionate to the size of their share holding, has not remained confined to the co-operative sugar industry. Other groups of processing co-operatives in our country have followed this example. This applies particularly to the co-operative potato-flour industry and the co-operative strawboard industry, both types of co-operative that have undergone considerable development in the Netherlands and which, as far as we know, are not, or hardly ever, met with abroad.

In the foregoing remarks we have concentrated attention particularly on co-operatives that required a large amount of capital from their very beginning. Many co-operatives, however, which are now of large size and in which large amounts of capital are now invested, began on a very modest scale, which means that at the time they were set up little demand was made on the members for financial support.

We may think, for example, of a *local consumers' co-operative* running one or more grocer's shops. The customers pay cash in the shop for groceries bought. These groceries are, on the other hand, supplied by the wholesalers or manufacturers on credit terms. This means that in actual fact the stocks held in the shops are financed by the suppliers. If one adds to this the fact that the shop premises can be rented, so that any financing is mainly concerned with the stocks, we see how it is possible to found co-operatives on the basis of non-liability, without having to require members to pay more than a modest entrance fee on joining, as is done in the case of local consumers' co-operative societies.

Another example of the same thing is provided by the *first purchasing co-operative* in our country, which confined itself originally to the co-operative purchase of fertilizer. As was explained in chapter III, this co-operative operated on an extremely simple basis, there being no need for any working capital at all. This co-operative, too, was able to do business without difficulty, without any capital being subscribed and without its members having to accept any financial liability on its behalf.

In the case of *other co-operatives*—insofar as their founding required some working capital, though only a modest amount—the founders had the choice either of providing this themselves or of borrowing it. Since, generally speaking, the first method of financing the enterprise met with difficulties as soon as sums of any size were involved—for most co-operatives were founded by those with few financial means—the two possibilities have generally been combined. That is to say, the members contributed a modest sum and at the same time accepted collective liability for the co-operative's commitments. On the founding of the first co-operatives in other sectors, however, unlimited liability was, in general, accepted as a matter of course, as it were, out of a sense of collective responsibility for affairs undertaken on a co-operative basis. Money could be borrowed on the basis of the collective financial liability of the members, whether limited to a certain amount or not, and such loans were gradually redeemed by regarding the sums necessary for the purpose as working costs. Account was taken of these working costs, which included interest and write-off, in determining the prices the co-operative paid its members for goods delivered to it and the prices charged to members for farm equipment delivered to them.

This principle, moreover, was not only applied to build up surpluses to pay off the co-operative's debts but was also used to form its own capital, so that by means of this price policy the necessary write-offs and reserves were obtained. The formation of the co-operative's own capital which came about in this manner did not, however, assume sufficient proportions to enable the co-operatives to dispense entirely with borrowing long-term capital. On the contrary, even today the situation in many co-operatives is such that their own capital holdings must be regarded as too small compared with the total amount of long-term capital required. The fact that it has been possible on the basis of the members' liability to obtain this credit on easy terms has no doubt to do with this state of affairs.

We mentioned a moment ago that the first agricultural purchasing societies were set up without their having any capital of their own and without any liability on the part of the members. The later development of these purchasing co-operatives, as described in chapter III, soon brought about a marked increase in their capital requirements. This need was met partly by their forming their own fund of capital and partly by loans, the latter being made possible by reason of the fact that their members accepted a sufficient degree of liability. This liability is virtually unlimited in this sector as well.

In the case of the consumers' co-operatives, on the other hand, developments which have led to an increased demand for working capital (cf. chapter VI) have not resulted in any deviation from the principle of non-liability. In this sector, too, capital holdings have been built up by abstaining from distributing all the surplus among the members and by reserving part of it and investing it in the undertaking. This does not alter the fact that the consumers' co-operatives are also dependent on borrowed money for a large part of the working capital they require. The credit requirements of local consumers' co-operatives are supplied by the central organisation, except in so far as this need is met by credit granted by the suppliers of the goods dealt in. In its financial policy the central organisation has concentrated on the building up of its own capital, though this organisation also operates with loan money, borrowed partly on the basis of mortgage and partly on the basis of the confidence lenders have in the future of this co-operative enterprise.

The *farmers' credit banks* have gradually assumed an ever increasing share in the granting of credit to the co-operatives. They did, it is true, have a share in debenture loans issued by local co-operatives in the first phase of the development of the co-operative movement, and they also supplied bank loans to meet the need for short-term credit. Originally, however, their part in financing co-operatives was a modest one. Thanks to the favourable development of co-operative credit in our country, the farmers' credit banks have gradually been able to extend the scope of their financial assistance to co-operatives. Ever larger surpluses of deposits and savings over outstanding loans have been formed at these banks. Although the principles of good banking policy must be respected and although particular attention must be paid to liquidity, the latter is now so great in the case of the farmers' credit banks in our country that part of the available balances can be utilised to finance the co-operatives without involving any risk.

Agricultural credit institutions have not in the meantime restricted the granting of credit to short-term credit. The stronger the position of the farmers' credit banks and the more stability the co-operatives eligible for credit have displayed, the more ready credit institutions have gradually become to lend the co-operatives credit of a long-term character. Investment in factory equipment has been the main object of such loans. In judging this policy of the co-operative banks, it should be borne in mind that in granting credit to co-operatives, the central banks aimed particularly at stimulating co-operative activity.

It has already been pointed out in chapter II that the local farmers' credit banks restrict their lending to co-operatives of a local character.

The central banks play an important role in the financing of large —national and regional—co-operatives. These co-operatives also make a call on the capital market by issuing debenture loans.

In our foregoing remarks we have already indicated that, however attractive a basis unlimited liability may be for the granting of credit to co-operatives, it has the disadvantage of hampering the building up of the co-operatives' *own* fund of *capital.* This is also impeded by the fact that the co-operatives also need, of course, to be able to charge their members competitive prices.

It has long been realised in co-operative circles that it is essential for sound financing that the co-operatives should have a sufficient fund of their own capital to meet their long-term capital requirements. The question of building up the co-operatives' own fund of capital attracted much attention in co-operative circles even in the years prior to the second world war.

The war years, which witnessed a marked decline in turnover, were, however, very unfavourable for building up the co-operatives' capital and after the war it was primarily the government's fiscal policy that restricted this. The heavier the taxation imposed on capital increments, the less one was ready to build up capital reserves.

An attempt has been made—avoiding fiscal objections—to meet the co-operatives' capital requirements by the system of "members' accounts", though this did not contribute to the formation of the co-operatives' own capital. According to this system credit balances were not paid out in their entirety to members straightaway. Instead, part of each member's share was credited to a special account opened in his name. Although these balances are transferred in this way into the member's possession, the members can only dispose of the sum on their account under certain circumstances, for instance, when they reach a certain age, when they close down their business, when they move elsewhere, etc. As these balances remain at the society's disposal for some time, it can use them as its working capital. Since there is a transfer of ownership, the amounts credited to the members' accounts cannot be taxed as part of the co-operative's capital; they represent members' income and are taxable only under income tax regulations. Since the rate of income tax, however, is generally lower than the rate of company tax, the procedure followed is advantageous both to the co-operative and to the body of its members.

chapter XI

The co-operative movement
and the government

The foregoing chapters have made it clear that the origin and growth of the co-operative movement in the Netherlands have been of spontaneous character, the government having exercised practically no influence on the movement's development. It should be borne in mind, however, that most co-operative societies in our country were founded before the first world war, that is to say, in a period when governments pursued a policy of *non-intervention*. Moreover, the state cannot easily side with the co-operative movement as this would often mean siding against the middle class of shopkeepers and the owners of small businesses, who are large in number in a densely populated country like ours. This controversy, which, by the way, occurs in only a few branches, is very likely the reason why it is also customary for the political parties to avoid any positive statement of views on co-operation. Finally, an important factor is that once it had made good progress, the co-operative movement had no need for government assistance. Government assistance is inconceivable without government influence and the members of the co-operative movement in the Netherlands want to remain themselves.

Typical of the government's passive attitude towards the co-operative movement is the fact that the first co-operatives in our country were set up before any special act on co-operatives had been passed. This was possible, since they could be set up under an act of 1855 relating to associations in general. This act is still in force and although there has been *a special Co-operative Societies Act* in our country since 1876, numerous co-operatives have been set up since then under the 1855 act, instead of under the act of 1876. It makes little difference in practice, though a co-operative founded under the Co-operative Societies Act must include the term "co-operative" in its title, which obligation is not incumbent on a society operating on a co-operative basis and founded under the 1855 act.

An explanation for the fact that in our country co-operatives are based on different acts can be found in the *definition* contained in the Co-operative Societies Act of 1876, which is still in force, having been

Co-operatives are promoting the use of modern machinery

Artificial insemination has become of great importance nowadays

The success of the co-operative movement depends in the last resort on the people themselves: it is up to them

amended in 1925. According to this definition, co-operative societies must be taken to include: "associations the members of which are free to join or leave the association, and the aim of which is to promote the members' material interests, such as by means of the joint exercise of their trade or craft, by procurement of their requisites or by supplying them with advances or credit". The act also states that: "An association which fulfils these requirements does not lose its character, if its statutes permit it to extend the scope of its activities to third persons, nor if it promotes other interests besides material ones".

Thus the Co-operative Societies Act gives pride of place to the promotion of *material interests*. For this reason, however, the founders of co-operatives, whose prime aim was the promotion of the non-material interests of their members—even though they sought to achieve this by carrying on business—preferred the 1855 act, which generally speaking is intended for societies with non-economic aims. This difference in emphasis was partly the reason why it was decided to set up two central farmers' credit banks, whereby two distinctly separate groups of credit co-operatives have come into being in our country.

In the meantime the Netherlands government has presented proposals to parliament regarding a wholesale reform of the civil code. Should these proposals be accepted, in future it will only be possible to found co-operatives according to provisions contained in the new civil code. The criterion for a co-operative will again be whether the society's aim is to promote certain material interests of its members. This in no way means, however, that a co-operative society will not be able to set itself any aim other than a material one, but it will mean that, in order to be a co-operative in the sense of the legislative proposals, it must carry on some business on its members' behalf. It is proposed to maintain the provision at present in force, obliging co-operative societies to include the term "co-operative" in their title.

As regards the Co-operative Societies Act of 1925, besides *provisions of a binding nature,* which must be observed in all circumstances, this act also contains *provisions which need not be adhered to,* if explicit mention of such divergence is made in the society's statutes. This system will undoubtedly be preserved in the new legislation.

The system has the advantage that certain fundamental principles must be applied in all circumstances, though, on the other hand, sufficient latitude is allowed for adapting the statutes to the highly varied circumstances under which different co-operatives work; for the concept of the "co-operative" is a complex one, covering many types of widely divergent society.

A few examples are given below of provisions in the Co-operative Societies Act which have to be observed in all circumstances.

The Co-operative Societies Act makes it *compulsory* for a co-operative society to state clearly in its statutes the name of the co-operative and of the municipality in which it is established, together with the nature of the business it is engaged in. In addition the statutes must contain rules concerning the financial liability of the members towards their society and a clause making clear the procedure to be followed, should it be decided to bring about any change in the statutes.

The Co-operative Societies Act also provides that applications for membership of a co-operative society must always be made in writing and that the reply to such applications must likewise be in writing. The act expressly provides, however, that should this obligation not be observed, the absence of a document cannot be taken as proof of non-membership. If a member has always behaved as a member, he is regarded as being one.

The Co-operative Societies Act next provides that a general meeting must be held, if requested by at least one fifth of the members. Should the board fail to respond to this request, the members making the request can convene a meeting themselves.

The Co-operative Societies Act provides that the board must be elected by the members and that the members can dismiss the board at any time.

The act also provides that a general meeting must be held annually, at which meeting the board must present a report and statement of accounts, supported by the necessary documents, relative to its conduct of the society's business.

Now a few examples of *provisions* in the Co-operative Societies Act *which need not be adhered to,* provided this is expressly stated in the *statutes.* This condition is clearly one of importance, for it obliges the members to declare their attitude on such points, if they should decide to set up a co-operative or to modify an existing co-operative's statutes.

The act provides inter alia:

Insofar as the statutes do not provide otherwise, membership of a co-operative is a personal matter, which means, for instance, that if a member of a co-operative dies, his son who takes over the farm or business cannot automatically be regarded as a member of the co-operative. This provision also makes it possible, moreover, for corporations (co-operatives, limited companies, etc.) to be members of a co-operative society.

Unless it is determined otherwise in the statutes, each member of a co-operative has one vote at the general meeting. Thus this provision implies that members can under certain circumstances have more than one vote

Unless the statutes otherwise determine, the board of a co-operative

90

consists of five persons, who appoint from among their number a chairman, a secretary and a treasurer.

If supervision of the management of the co-operative is not provided for in the statutes, the general meeting appoints a committee of three each year to examine the board's report and statement of accounts, —assisted, if necessary, by one or two experts—and to report to the general meeting on their findings.

Unless the statutes otherwise determine, the members of a co-operative and those who were members at any time during the preceding year have unlimited liability for equal shares of any deficit of the society.

In this respect it should be mentioned that the act distinguishes three possibilities as regards regulations concerning liability. These are: a) the liability prescribed in the act, i.e. unlimited liability; b) a liability diverging from that laid down in the act and which is usually more limited; and c) non-liability. The members of a co-operative are free to decide which they prefer, but their choice must be indicated by adding to the society's name the letters W.A. (in Dutch: wettelijke aansprakelijkheid, i.e. that laid down in the act), G.A. (gewijzigde aansprakelijkheid, i.e. modified liability) 1) or U.A. (uitgesloten aansprakelijkheid, i.e. non-liability). Such indication is for the information of others. Moreover, the act provides that a copy of the statutes and of the annual balance and trading account must be deposited with the Chamber of Commerce.

One more provision in the Co-operative Societies Act needs to be mentioned, that concerning the *members' council*. The act provides that should the number of members exceed two hundred, the co-operative's statutes may prescribe that the general meeting should consist of a council, elected by the members, of at least twenty members, and that the method of their election must be laid down in the statutes.

The need for such a provision in the act is clear. There are societies with thousands, some with tens of thousands of members. Naturally, a general meeting of members of this size could never answer the purpose. Nevertheless, a board must be elected and its conduct of the co-operative's business examined every year. This could be done by a referendum, but it is often better for the members to set up a representative body which can exercise the function normally intended to be excercised by

---

1) In contrast to the provision in the act, which involves unlimited liability for equal shares in any deficit, this allows of the possibility of arriving at a regulation, whereby each member bears unlimited liability *individually*. This latter form of liability, which accordingly goes further than that prescribed in the act, must be indicated by the letters G.A., which, however, usually indicate a liability of more limited nature than that laid down in the act.

the general meeting. This body, known as the members' council, accordingly acts in the place of the general meeting.

Various large co-operatives in the Netherlands make use of the possibility thus provided by the act and in many cases the system works satisfactorily. A disadvantage of the system is that direct contact between individual members and the co-operative is weakened and this is why other co-operatives with several hundreds of members do not wish to have a members' council. It is very often the custom of these co-operatives to call regional meetings of members, which meetings are regarded as a means to sound the members' opinions before the general meeting is held. In this way it is possible to turn the general meeting into a congress without losing its real function. This is one of the reasons why the setting up of a members' council is not made compulsory in the act, should the number of members of a co-operative exceed a certain figure [1]).

Finally it should be mentioned that the Co-operative Societies Act contains a provision obliging every co-operative to call in the assistance of an appropriately qualified representative of the government, i.e. a *notary,* when framing or modifying its statutes. This notary must see that the statutes fulfil reasonable requirements and accord with general legislation.

We have already pointed out that, in general, the co-operative movement in the Netherlands receives no aid from the government. It is desirable to say something here about the *government's taxation policy.*

For the purpose of taxation the co-operative is treated in the same way in the Netherlands as the limited company. This means, inter alia, that the co-operative, too, is subject to the provisions of the Company Tax Act, which lays down the rules for calculating the amount of tax due.

We should not have touched on this subject, were it not for the fact that many not kindly inclined towards the co-operative movement draw the conclusion from the manner in which company tax provisions are applied to the concept of "profit" that the co-operatives are accorded a privileged position and consequently receive financial support, a conclusion which representatives of the co-operative movement categorically reject.

Insofar as the concept of profit is put on a par with the concept of an increase in capital holdings, no difference of opinion is possible.

---

[1]) Also in the case of a members' council, which precludes the existence of a general meeting, an attempt is sometimes made to meet the objection mentioned above, by holding regional meetings which are open to all individual members and at which the members of the said council are elected. It is clear that no decisions can be taken at these regional meetings.

92

But when it comes to the question of whether a credit balance on the trading account should also be regarded as profit insofar as this is distributed among the members—either in cash or in the form of a credit to their "member's account"—the views of the protagonists and opponents of the co-operative movement display wide divergence. The opponents of the movement apply a simple line of reasoning. They regard the favourable balance distributed among members as profit, pure and simple, and therefore as taxable. Those associated with the co-operative movement, however, take the view that periodic settlements of accounts with members are provisional in character, for to begin with the co-operative employs "advance" prices, and it is only at the end of the financial year that the account can be finally made up, which means that it is only then that it is ascertained whether these temporary prices were accurate or not. The distribution among members of balances built up during the year accordingly bears the character of an adjustment. Naturally, one remains on the safe side when calculating the provisional prices and making the advance settlements, for it would be highly undesirable to have to inform members at the end of the year that the advance prices the co-operative had reckoned for goods delivered and services rendered to them had been too low or that it had paid them too high a price for products put at its disposal, so that the co-operative now had a claim upon them. It is far more efficient—and more pleasant—to be able to distribute a surplus at the year's end.

Nevertheless, it cannot be denied that the problem is more complicated than might appear from the above. This becomes clear particularly when one takes into account that in many cases co-operatives do business with non-members, a possibility provision for which is made in the Co-operative Societies Act. Insofar as a profit is made on business transacted with non-members, it must be conceded that such profit is taxable, which fact is also accepted by co-operators generally.

Finally, some mention of the position the co-operative movement occupies in the field of *education* and in the *agricultural extension (advice) service*.

As regards the latter, it follows from what has already been said earlier on in this chapter that in furnishing advice on agriculture, the government does not make any propaganda for the co-operative movement, since here, too, a policy of neutrality must be observed. This neutrality does not go so far as to preclude mention of the word "co-operation" by the agriculture extension service or to preclude officials employed by the service from having their own opinion on co-operatives. In actual fact many agricultural consultants (extension officers) are convinced of the great importance of co-operation, while there are others who favour private enterprise. This does not give

93

rise to any difficulty, however, since the work of agricultural consultants is primarily of a technical nature.

Naturally the necessary attention is devoted to the co-operative movement in education, for the movement plays a significant role in the economic life of our country. This is particularly the case in agricultural education. The co-operative movement forms part of the curriculum not only at the lower and secondary agricultural schools but also at institutes of higher education. It is true that there is no separate chair of agricultural co-operation at the National College of Agriculture at Wageningen, but this subject is dealt with by the professor in agricultural economics.

A special chair of co-operation in general was set up in 1941 in the faculty of economics at the University of Amsterdam, which step was taken in consultation with and with the co-operation of the National Co-operative Council.

chapter XII

Conclusion

The term *co-operation covers a multitude of different forms.* The picture we have sketched of the co-operative movement in the Netherlands affords us a clear illustration of this. It is not only that various groups of interested persons (farmers, market gardeners, shopkeepers, owners of small businesses, consumers) have formed themselves into co-operatives, acting independently of one another; there is also the fact that in the case of the agricultural co-operative especially, a large number of different forms can be distinguished, according to the aim the founders had in view when they set up the co-operative. Moreover, co-operatives in the different sectors of social life have met with varying degrees of success, which has influenced the outward form of their organisation; this indeed, shows marked variation, since the same need was not felt in every sector of co-operative life for a transfer of authority to the central organisations. Finally, the composite character of the co-operative movement is also expressed in the considerable variation found in the internal organisation of different co-operatives .

Anyone endeavouring to form an idea of the origin and development of the co-operative movement and attempting to come to an opinion as to the desirability of setting up new co-operative societies or the possibility of developing existing ones, should keep the complex character of the co-operatives particularly in mind. In doing so, he will come to the conclusion that the different circumstances in which the various types of co-operatives work provide an explanation of the great variety the movement displays. This does not apply exclusively to the Netherlands but to all countries in which co-operation has been left free to develop along its own lines.

Notwithstanding the limited degree of uniformity which also characterises the co-operative movement in the Netherlands, it is possible to draw a *few general conclusions.* There is all the more reason for doing so, since it has been necessary in this work to deal with the various forms of co-operative in separate chapters.

In the first place it can be stated that the setting-up of co-operatives is dependent on a *comparison between the interests* the members might have in such a co-operative *and the risks* it would involve. For instance, whereas farmers whose existence depended entirely on the price of milk found no difficulty in deciding to found a co-operative dairy factory, the same cattle farmers did not prove willing to found a co-operative shoe factory in order to be able to obtain better prices for the hides of their slaughter cattle.

In considering the co-operative movement in the Netherlands, it must also be remembered that the founding of the first co-operatives was a *spontaneous* process and that no preconceived plan was followed, when founding subsequent co-operatives. This is to be explained first and foremost by the fact that the first co-operatives were founded in a period in which the "laissez faire, laissez aller" principle was believed in, and when there was no question of any state interference in economic affairs. In order to bring about an improvement in their unfavourable social position—which was due chiefly to their comparatively weak bargaining position on the market—various economic groups decided to found co-operative societies; for the founding of the first co-operatives was a reaction to certain abuses, such as sharp practice, adulteration, exorbitant rates of interest, the setting up of monopolies etc., the aim of the farmers and market gardeners being to restore equilibrium on the market.

The success of the first co-operatives caused other to follow the example of the pioneers on a large scale, so that a network of co-operative societies soon came into existence, bringing about a great improvement in the position of those concerned. It can be said without any doubt at all that co-operative activity has developed on a scale its founders had never foreseen. Although in later periods co-operative societies have repeatedly been set up when there was no definite abuse to counter, in general, the movement must still be regarded today as a *corrective* to unequal bargaining positions on the market. This corrective is undoubtedly just as necessary today to counter the great concentration of power in the form of modern cartels and trusts, as it was in the days of free competition.

The view that the co-operative movement must be seen primarily as a corrective certainly applies to the consumers' co-operatives in our country, too. Although the first consumers' co-operatives laid the emphasis on bringing about a change in the social order, nowadays this co-operative socialism finds scarcely any support in consumers' co-operative circles in the Netherlands. Today the prime aim of the consumers' co-operatives, too, is to supply their members with good quality produce at as low a price as possible. And in our country as well they have not been content to seek to achieve this aim solely by assuming the role of wholesalers, but have also taken to manufacturing certain articles themselves.

The history of the co-operative movement in the Netherlands— which displays a great deal of resemblance to that in other countries, European countries particularly—leads one to the conclusion that, if a co-operative society is to succeed, certain *conditions* must be fulfilled.

In the first place, the *social structure of the population* has shown itself to be a factor of great importance. It can be said without doubt that the greater the social distinction between the inhabitants of a village or district, or between the members of a given group, the more difficult it proves to found a co-operative. The fact that in the Netherlands social differences in rural areas are, generally speaking, very slight—at least compared with other countries—is one of the reasons for the readiness shown by the more wel-to-do to lend the credit co-operatives their support. They were conscious of a feeling of solidarity with their fellow villagers and fellow farmers, and this persuaded them to join the co-operative and thereby to accept unlimited liability for the society's commitments, which meant that the society won sufficient confidence as a savings bank.

Generally speaking, a *sense of solidarity* among those intending to set up a co-operative and among the members of an existing co-operative must be regarded as a highly important factor. The possibility of a co-operative's further progress is largely dependent on the perseverance that the members, generally, and the board, in particular, are capable of demonstrating. This is particularly important when it comes to carrying on the struggle they consciously accepted when founding the co-operative, and when their first efforts do not immediately lead to the desired results. In the early stages particularly, when the young co-operative is still financially weak and when it has not yet proved its viability, its opponents—who fear that nothing but disadvantage will result for them from its successful development—will not hesitate to make things as difficult as they can for it. They will not even shrink from boycotting it. Limitations of space have made it impossible in this work to give a full description of the struggle many young co-operatives have had to go through; the reader may be sure, however, that, generally speaking, the path the co-operative pioneers had to tread was no easy one, and that it often required a great deal of perseverance to ensure the co-operative's success. In carrying on such a struggle, it is of the greatest importance that one should be able to rely on the loyalty of the co-operative's members.

But however important a sense of solidarity may be, a co-operative must, of course, have *sufficient financial resilience*. Since most co-operatives were founded by persons with few financial resources of their own, the first co-operatives particularly had to rely on loans, the basis for which was the members' liability—often unlimited—sometimes combined with an obligation to make use of their co-operative under all circumstances. It is obvious that even in employing this method of financing, certain minimum requirements were necessary as regards the members' financial position, and this was especially so in the early stages. Once a co-operative has developed so far, main attention has to be devoted to building up its own capital holdings. Co-operatives requiring a good deal of capital investment must dispose of a reasonable amount of their own capital from the very beginning, and this applies all the more strongly the less prepared the members are to accept liability themselves.

Of vital significance for the success of a co-operative is, moreover, the *quality of its leaders.* This does not apply to the board members alone, but also—and perhaps primarily—to its managers, who are in charge of the daily conduct of business on the board's behalf. The leaders of the first co-operatives had enjoyed little education and had no experience of managing a business. They were, however, men of strong personality, endowed with a large measure of common sense, and they enjoyed the confidence of the members, thanks chiefly to their integrity. Moreover, they were often born managers and propagandists and were inspired by a social ideal to which they were ready to devote themselves wholeheartedly. Since the first co-operatives were set up, the management of a business—and of a co-operative—has become a much more complicated affair, and the management of large regional and "top" co-operatives particularly calls for managers and directors of great capacity. But some training for managers and executives of the local co-operatives is also of the greatest importance and increasing attention ought accordingly to be given to this matter.

But even when a co-operative is efficiently led, an effective super-vision of the administration and of the board's organisational policy remains essential. Once the co-operative has assumed any size, the general meeting or the supervisory council, which is entrusted with the task of supervising the board's management on the general meeting's behalf, is not able to carry out such control without expert assistance. In the absence of thorough audit and examination of the administration, disappointments are unavoidable This is all the more difficult, because the failure of a co-operative would lead to undesirable reactions of an irreparable nature among the members of other co-operatives. Although one can hardly talk of the co-operative movement as a homogeneous whole, such failure would put an easy weapon in the hands of its enemies for the purpose of carrying on propaganda against this form of enterprise.

In our country the *central organisations,* formed by groups of similar co-operatives, play an important role. Generally speaking, although the amount of authority local co-operatives have transferred to central organisations varies from sector to sector, these central organisations have had a favourable influence on the development of the co-operative movement. They perform valuable services for their member organisations of an organisational, technical, economic, legal and administrative nature. An important feature in this respect is the fact that many central organisations have set up an inspection service, which carries out periodic audits of the administration and bookkeeping of local co-operatives. This not only provides the individual members of the co-operatives concerned with the certainty that they can rely on the information the board puts before their general meeting, it also makes it possible for the central organisation itself to keep an eye on the course things are taking in each of its members co-operatives. In such cases, by becoming members of the central organisation, the local co-operatives assume the obligation to use the services of the inspection department. This often means that in organising their own bookkeeping, they must follow the lines laid down by the central organisation. It can also mean that some of the decisions they take are subject to the central organisation's approval, e.g. in the case of the appointment of a manager.

Whilst recognising the great merits of various forms of co-operation in the past, one may ask *what the significance of the co-operative movement is today*. That the movement in our country is an important social phenomenon is obvious at first sight. It occupies an important place in the various sectors of economic activity, and, as can be seen from some figures quoted in this work, is sometimes even of greater significance than non-co-operative activity. The fact alone that there are more than 5,000 co-operatives in the Netherlands, with more than 45,000 employees, provides an illustration of the movement's size. The movement's social significance cannot, moreover, be deduced from figures alone.

The great importance of co-operation must, indeed, be sought first and foremost in its corrective effect on the lack of *equilibrium in market relationships*. The fact alone that economic groups occupying a weak bargaining position on the market have joined forces, has brought about an improvement in this respect. Since non-members as well as members of co-operatives have benefited as a result, the significance of the co-operative society goes beyond that of an organisation solely concerned with promoting the interests of its members.

Another important factor is the co-operative's aim to *promote its members' long-term interests*. The principle of payment according to quality can be mentioned here. The application of this principle by the co-operative dairy factories has made it possible to determine differences in the quality of milk yielded by different types of dairy cow, and this information is taken into good account in selecting cattle for breeding purposes. Later on, farmers outside the co-operative field also set up similar milk inspection associations. Further examples could be given of initiatives taken by the co-operative movement which competing con-

99

cerns were later obliged to imitate. Moreover, in many cases the aim the co-operative sets itself goes beyond the immediate one of promoting the interests of its own members. The attitude adopted by the central farmers' credit banks towards the financing of agricultural co-operatives, for instance, definitely goes further than an endeavour to serve the interests of members of the joint farmers' credit banks. The aim is rather to promote co-operative activity generally. The co-operative dairy factories also had wider aims in view when, working in collaboration with the herd books, they took the initiative in arriving at a systematic campaign to fight contagious diseases among cattle. Working together with members of agricultural organisations, representatives of the co-operatives have also repeatedly urged the government authorities to take legislative measures in the interests of groups of agricultural producers. It is also the declared aim of the consumers' co-operatives to serve the general interest as far as possible.

The fact that co-operative activity also aims at the promotion of the long-term interests of members must also be taken as the reason why the co-operatives provide *advice and information* on so wide a scale. Agricultural co-operatives, for instance, have done much to promote the efficient use of artificial fertilizers and feedstuffs, co-operative horticultural auctions have exercised a favourable influence on the manner in which vegetables and fruit are delivered, and co-operative dairy factories have worked untiringly for improved milk yields. All this has led to better results being obtained in agriculture. The information the consumers' co-operatives supply to their members causes housewives to pay more attention to the various uses to which they can put their housekeeping money, and this makes an indirect contribution towards a higher standard of living.

Of no less importance is the fact that for many people active participation in the co-operative movement brings with it a *widening of their mental horizon*. This applies to the members, who are required to express an opinion every year on the board's conduct of the society, and still more so to those who are called upon to lead the co-operatives. Formerly, for instance, farmers and market gardeners had only to concern themselves with matters to do with their own farms or undertakings. Membership of a co-operative society, however, confronts them with problems with which they previously did not come into contact. A widening of mental horizons lays the foundations for a broader general education, and this, in its turn, influences the farmers' readiness to accept new methods of agricultural production.

It has already been remarked that the co-operatives came into existence at a time when the state refrained from interfering in economic affairs. Since then a great change has come about. Free competition has been considerably restricted, especially by developments

100

in the technical field, and one of the results of this has been a change of view regarding the task of the government. Accordingly the state nowadays plays an important role in economic life and repeatedly takes action whenever there is any threat to the public interest. This economic policy involves weighing the interests of various economic groups against those of others, and a very important factor here is the amount of influence the groups concerned can bring to bear. In the present state of society it is not sufficient for agricultural producers to form themselves into agricultural organisations, for if they wish to represent their interests successfully, either with the government or with the organised employers or workers whom they meet around the conference table, they need to be experts not only in the agricultural field but also in the field of the marketing and processing of agricultural products. This *expertise* can be found among the leaders of agricultural co-operatives, who have concrete information at their disposal, without which all that could be said on behalf of the farmers and market gardeners would be remarks of a general nature, which, naturally enough, would not carry much conviction. The same applies to consumers' organisations, insofar as these are of a non-commercial character. There is no doubt that the consumers' co-operatives, working in the field of trade and production, are in a far better position to represent the interests of consumers.

Although the great significance of the co-operative movement as a social phenomenon may be generally admitted, nevertheless this form of enterprise is subject to *criticism*. This is understandable enough: there are two sides to every question, and no one, for example, will deny that the co-operative has often proved less able to come to decisions than have private undertakings and that a great deal of time and money has to be spent on meetings. The main objection to the co-operative movement, however, comes from groups who feel themselves threatened —we are thinking particularly of the owners of small businesses—people whose livelihoods are unfavourably affected by the expanding activities of the co-operatives. For this reason we do not think we need go into such criticism. Many shopkeepers have, as a matter of fact, long ago come to the conclusion that they, too, can best serve their own interests by applying the co-operative principle. The existence of various co-operatives among this group is a proof of this. Moreover, the co-operative movement has provided many with manual employment, in this way offering compensation for any loss of employment that may have occurred owing to the disappearance of small businesses. Another factor of vital importance is the question as to which form of enterprise performs the greatest service to society generally and from the favourable progress the co-operative movement has made it may be concluded that it serves a social need.

If, finally, we ask ourselves what *desiderata* still exist as regards the co-operative movement, as it has developed in the Netherlands, we would reply as follows.

In the first place it cannot be denied that there are still too many co-operatives which are too small in size from the economic point of view, and that in various sectors they could be run on more economic lines, if small local co-operatives could be amalgamated to form larger units. For since these small co-operatives were set up, many things have happened to make larger units more desirable. We need only point to the perfection of transport and to the large amount of capital investment that is nowadays required in the modern factory as a result of technical inventions. Greater capital investment results in higher overhead costs, which necessitate larger turnovers and consequently a wider field of operation. There can be no doubt at all that during the last few decades there has also been a great advance in *concentration* in the co-operative sector. The fact that this development has not led to entirely satisfactory results is to be ascribed chiefly to insufficient realisation of the truth that union is strength and too great an attachment to what has been achieved within a small compass.

Another problem that is demanding more attention is the *comparison of the results of different undertakings*. Such comparison is only possible if the bookkeeping and accounting of different undertakings are on the same lines. In order to arrive at uniformity in this respect, the collaboration of the boards of the co-operatives concerned is necessary. Here one often comes up against the difficulty that the boards are insufficiently informed on the subject of economics to be convinced of the need for comparing different undertakings.

In considering all these matters, one should not lose sight of the fact that the co-operative is the outcome of voluntary collaboration, and that even the relationship between the central organisations and their member co-operatives is based on voluntariness. Generally speaking, for this reason the co-operatives are undoubtedly less "go-ahead" than the large concerns. The large private concerns are also often quicker in taking decisions than are groups of co-operatives joined together in a central organisation. On the other hand, it must be stated that the voluntary nature of co-operation is one of its surest cornerstones. If the movement were to abandon this principle, it would lose one of its essential characteristics.

It has already been said more than once here that the further progress of the co-operative movement stands or falls on the quality of its leaders. Although in many cases the manager of a co-operative has left his own personal stamp on the undertaking, a co-operative's progress is particularly dependent upon the quality of its board, and its chairman especially. It must be stated that there is a great shortage of reliable and capable board members in the Netherlands, too, and this is why a great deal of attention is being paid to the *training* of men for this purpose.

Although the co-operative movement has made sound progress in the Netherlands practically without any help from the government—here we leave out of account the subsidy until recently granted to agricultural machinery co-operatives, since this is an exception from which no general conclusion can be drawn—this certainly does not mean that co-operation excludes all *government influence as a matter of principle*. In France, for instance, the government helps to meet the need for agricultural credit. This it endeavours to do by fostering the farmers' credit banks. In Italy, too, where a reform of agriculture is taking place, the authorities giving the lead try to stimulate the farmers' own efforts by founding co-operatives. Even the federal government in the U.S.A. promotes co-operation in agriculture. This appears to be a contradiction to the principle of free competition, which, generally speaking, is the ideal followed in that country. The influence the government brings to bear in this respect, however, results from its wish to achieve a balance of power in the markets for agrarian produce and agricultural requisites. As regards the under-developed countries outside Europe, it is generally accepted in these countries, too, that it lies with their governments to give powerful support to co-operation.